Lydia Maria Francis Child, William Grant Sewell

The Right Way the Safe Way

Proved by emancipation in the British West Indies, and elsewhere

Lydia Maria Francis Child, William Grant Sewell

The Right Way the Safe Way
Proved by emancipation in the British West Indies, and elsewhere

ISBN/EAN: 9783337316280

Printed in Europe, USA, Canada, Australia, Japan

Cover: Foto ©Suzi / pixelio.de

More available books at **www.hansebooks.com**

THE RIGHT WAY THE SAFE WAY,

PROVED BY

EMANCIPATION IN THE BRITISH WEST INDIES,
AND ELSEWHERE.

BY L. MARIA CHILD.

"The world is beginning to understand, that injuring one class, for the immediate benefit of another, is ultimately injurious to that other; and that to secure prosperity to a community, *all* interests must be consulted."—*Dr. Davy.*

NEW YORK:
PUBLISHED AND FOR SALE AT 5 BEEKMAN STREET.
1862.

CHAPTER I.

THE WEST INDIES BEFORE THE ABOLITION OF SLAVERY.

It is a common idea that the British West Indies were a mine of wealth before the abolition of slavery, and since that event have been sinking into ruin. To correct those erroneous impressions, I have carefully collected the following facts from authentic sources: —

Official Reports, returned to the British Parliament, prove that the outcry about ruin in the West Indies began *long before* the abolition of slavery, and even before the abolition of the slave *trade;* and we ought, moreover, never to forget that this outcry related solely to the ruin of the *masters;* nobody expended a thought upon the ruin of their 800,000 laborers.

As early as 1792, a Report to Parliament stated that, in the course of the preceding twenty years, one hundred and seventy-seven estates in Jamaica had been sold for the payment of debts; the cultivation of fifty-five had been abandoned; ninety-two were in the hands of creditors; and 80,021 executions, amounting to £22,500,000 sterling ($109,012,500), had been lodged in the provost marshal's office. In 1805, the Reports described the condition of the West India planters as one of "increasing embarrassment, and impending ruin." The Reports in 1807, 1808, 1812, 1830, and 1832, were still more lamentable. In 1830, four years before emancipation, Lord Chandos presented to Parliament a petition from West India planters and merchants, setting forth "the extreme distress under which they labored." In his speech, in support of the petition, he said, "They are reduced to a state in which they are obliged earnestly to solicit relief from Parliament. It is not possible for them to stand up against such a pressure any longer."
Mr. Bright said: "The distress of the West India Colonies

is unparalleled in the country. Many families, who formerly
lived in comparative affluence, are reduced to absolute penury." The West India Reporter also quoted thus from a Report on the commercial state of the Colonies: "There are
strong concurrent testimonies and proofs that, unless some
speedy and efficient measures of relief are adopted, the ruin
of a great number of the planters must inevitably take place."
An able writer in the *Edinburgh Review* informs us that,
"In the small island of St. Lucia an Encumbered Estate
Court was established in 1833, and, small as that island is,*
in the first eighteen months, liabilities were recorded to the
enormous amount of £1,089,965 ($5,280,880); *all debts incurred under slavery.* Nor did that island stand alone. In
each one of them the same state of things prevailed." The
laborers were decreasing rapidly. The *Edinburgh Review*
declares: "What gave the death-blow to slavery, in the minds
of British statesmen, was the appalling fact that the Population Returns, from only eleven of the Colonies, showed
that, in the course of twelve years, the slaves had decreased
60,219. Had similar returns been procured from the other
seven Colonies, they must have shown a decrease of little, if
at all, less than 100,000. Had the same rate of decrease
gone on, one century would have seen the extinction of slavery by the extinction of the slaves."† Production was also
decreasing. A table of exports, in the Appendix to Mr.
Bigelow's work on Jamaica, shows that, in the ten years ending 1830, there was a decrease in that island, of 201,843
hogsheads of sugar, from the amount in the ten years ending
with 1820. In view of these, and similar facts, the *Edinburgh Review* says: "Plainly, the artificial, arbitrary interference of law with the freedom of man, and freedom of
trade, was bringing about the extinction of the working-class,
and was whirling their masters along to utter ruin."

---

* It is about as large as eight common New England towns.
† It must not be inferred from this statement that the system of slavery was more cruel in the West Indies, than in other sugar-growing
Colonies and States. Wherever *sugar* is produced by slave-labor,
there is always an awful destruction of negro life, owing to the severely
hard pressure of work, continued night and day, during one particular
season of the crops.

At the time when the planters were complaining of such excessive embarrassments, they had a monopoly of the sugar market in Great Britain, so close that not even the East India Colonies were allowed to compete with them; a monopoly, which cost the comsumers $25,000,000 annually. They paid no wages to their laborers; and furnished them merely with rags to tie about their loins, and enough of coarse food to keep them in working condition. Yet while they produced from a prolific soil the great staples of commerce, without paying for the labor, and with an enormous premium from the consumers in Great Britain, they were so nearly reduced to "ruin," that they were compelled "earnestly to solicit relief from Parliament."

A few facts will help to explain this apparent anomaly. In the first place, the system of slavery contravenes all the laws of human nature, and therefore contains within itself the seed of ultimate ruin. It takes away the motive power from the laborers, who naturally desire to shirk as much as possible of the work, which brings them no pay; consequently, overseers and drivers must be hired to force out of them their unwilling toil. It makes them indifferent to the destruction of property on estates, in whose prosperity they have no interest. It stimulates them to theft, by perpetual privations, from which they have no prospect of relief. It kills their ingenuity and enterprise, by rendering them utterly unavailing for any improvement in their own condition; while all their faculties are stupefied by the extreme ignorance in which they must necessarily be kept in order to be held in slavery. The effects on the white population are quite as injurious, though in a different way. Slavery unavoidably renders labor a degradation, and consequently, it is a matter of pride with them to live in idleness. Extravagance and dissipation follow of course. All, who have examined into the subject, are aware that intemperance, licentiousness, and gambling, are fearfully prevalent in slaveholding countries. One hint will suffice to suggest the immoral condition of the West Indies, during slavery. It is a well-known fact that the white subordinates employed by planters were very liable to lose their situations if they married; because it was for the interest of the proprietors to have them live with slaves, and raise up laborers for the estates. As for the slaves, being regarded as animals, and treated like live-stock, they unavoidably lived like animals. Modesty and self-respect were impossible to their brutalized condition. In this Tract, I merely aim at presenting a *business*-view of the subject. Therefore, I will not describe the cruelties, which were continually practised, and which kept the worst passions of both masters and slaves in perpetual excitement. The barbarities recorded were the same that always *must* prevail, under a system of coerced labor and irresponsible power.

In addition to the unavoidable expenses, and inevitable deterioration involved in the very nature of slavery, the West India planters had another difficulty to contend with. " Nearly the whole of the sugar estates were owned by absentees, the greater part of whom never set foot in the islands." This involved the necessity of hiring managers and attorneys to look after the property. Mr. Bigelow computes the average annual expense of an estate to have been $3,000, solely to pay for the absence of the proprietor. The Rev. Henry Bleby, who was a missionary in the West Indies before emancipation, and has resided there ever since, says : " Let us look at the condition of a West India estate under slavery. There were four or five hundred slaves. True, there was little expended for their food; but their masters had to supply them with so many yards of cloth a year, and several other small articles. That was one item of expense. Then, to superintend the labor of these slaves, there must be four bookkeepers, as they were called ; one to superintend the still, another the boiling-house, another the cattle on the estate, and another, sometimes two or three others, to superintend the people in the field. All these had to be fed and salaried. Then there was the overseer, with his harem, living at considerable expense out of the estate, and at a high salary. Over all these was the attorney, who took his commission out of every thing the estate produced, and lived in the great house with his servants and harem. Then there was the proprietor living with his family in princely style, in France or England. All this was to be drawn out of the produce of one estate ! I should like to know whether there is any property that would not be brought to ruin, with so many living upon it, and out of it."

Everybody knows how property is cared for, when there are none but hirelings to look after it. All accounts of the West Indies abound with the complaints of proprietors concerning the neglect, wastefulness, and fraud of their subordinates. Accumulation of salaries being the principal object in view, one manager often superintended many estates. Dr. Davy, in his work on the West Indies, speaks of twenty-three estates in Montserrat, managed by one agent. He reports nineteen of them as "imperfectly cultivated," or "abandoned;" which is by no means surprising, under the circumstances. Mr. Bigelow met in Jamaica, a gentleman who had come from England to ascertain why he was always sinking more and more money upon his estate. Upon inquiry, he discovered that his manager lived sixty miles from the property, and had never seen it.

With such drains upon their income, the proprietors were, of course, obliged to borrow money continually. Year after year, a gambling game was carried on between them and the merchants of London. The merchant would advance money to the planter, on condition that all the produce of the estate should be consigned to his house, and that whatever was needed on the estate, in his line of business, should be bought of him. The merchant charged what price he pleased for his own articles, and took what commission he pleased for selling the produce. "Thus," says Mr. Bigelow, "the planter's candle was burning at both ends." If there was a hurricane, or a severe drought, or an insurrection of the slaves, which caused a failure of the crops, the proprietor was obliged to mortgage his lands to get the necessary supply of money. Thus a great many of the estates passed into the hands of British merchants, and had a heavy interest to pay in addition to other expenses.

Such was the state of things, when the British people, ignorant of this financial chaos, and actuated solely by motives of justice and humanity, started the idea of abolishing slavery. When the planters became aware that the measure might be carried, they met it with a furious storm of opposition. They characterized it as an "impertinent interference with their rights," and threatened to withdraw from the British government, unless the project were relinquished. Still they petitioned for relief; any kind of relief, except from the destructive system, which had brought them to the verge of ruin. To *that* they swore they never would submit. Missionaries, who went to the West Indies to impart religious instruction to the slaves, were assaulted with brickbats and imprisoned on false pretences. Their houses were attacked, and their chapels demolished. A Colonial Union was formed, the object of which was to drive away every instructor of the negroes. Those in England, who sought to help on the cause of emancipation, were hated with inconceivable intensity. Women in the West Indies expressed a wish to get hold of Wilberforce "that they might pull his heart out." With these wrathful vociferations were mingled every form of lamentable prediction concerning the ruin "fanatical philanthropists" were bringing on the Colonies. They said if their mad designs were carried into execution, the masters would all have their throats cut, and their houses burned. What they seemed especially concerned about was that "the negroes could not possibly take care of themselves." They were too lazy to work without the whip. They would abscond to the woods, and live there like animals. The few, who might be willing to work, would be robbed by the others; that would lead to continual fighting, and there would be prodigious slaughter. Thousands also would die of disease, from want of the fostering care of their masters. In short, blacks and whites would all be swallowed up in one great gulf of swift destruction.

The Colonial press was, of course, on the side of slavery. There was all manner of suppression of truth, and propagation of every sort of falsehood on the subject. But through all these obstacles, the work of reform went slowly and steadily on. It took twenty years of hard labor and violent agitation to abolish the slave-*trade;* then eleven years, still more stormy, to abolish the *system.* But, at last, the Act of Emancipation was passed, and went into effect in 1834. The slaves received nothing from the British government for centuries of unrequited toil. But £20,000,000 ($96,-900,000) were paid to the masters, for ceasing to extort labor by the lash. That was called Compensation. With the idea of preparing the bondmen for freedom, the Act of Emancipation was unfortunately clogged with an Apprenticeship System, by which it was ordained that the emancipated laborers were to work six years for their masters, without wages, as before. But they were to work nine hours a day, instead of twelve; and were to have half of Friday, and the whole of Saturday, for themselves. The power of punishing was also taken from masters, and transferred to magistrates. Household slaves were to become entirely free in 1838, and field slaves in 1840.

Men long accustomed to arbitrary power are not easily convinced that it is both right and politic to relinquish the exercise of it. Moreover, we are all, more or less, the creatures of custom and prejudice. Therefore, it is not surprising that the great body of the planters were opposed to emancipation, until the eventful crisis had actually passed. Up to the last month, they remonstrated, and threatened, and entreated the Home Government not to consign them to such inevitable destruction. Many judicious and kindly men among them thought otherwise. They were convinced that the present system was certainly bringing ruin upon the Colonies, and they felt persuaded that nothing worse could come in its place. Their belief in the safety of emancipation was partly founded upon general principles of human nature, and partly upon their experimental knowledge of the docility of the negroes, when justly and humanely treated. But very few of these individuals dared, however, to express such opinions; for the community was in such an excited state, that they were sure to suffer for it, in some form or other.

Mr. James Scotland, of St. John's, Antigua, said to Mr. Thome: "Whoever was known or suspected of being an advocate for freedom, became an object of vengeance, and was sure to suffer by a loss of business, if in no other way. Every attempt was made to deprive my son of business, as a lawyer; and I was thrown into prison, without any form of trial, or any opportunity of saying one word in my own defence. There I remained, till discharged by the peremptory orders of the Colonial Secretary, to whom I appealed for relief. The opinions of the clergymen and missionaries, with the exception of a few of the clergy, were favorable to emancipation; but neither in their conduct, preaching, nor prayers, did they declare themselves openly, until the measure of abolition was determined on. The missionaries felt restrained by their instructions from home; and the clergy thought it did not comport with their order to take part in politics. I never heard of a single planter, who was favorable, until about three months before emancipation took place; when some few of them began to perceive that it would be advantageous to their interest."

Mr. Thome, in his work on the West Indies, says: "We were informed that, some time previous to the abolition of slavery, a meeting of the influential men in Antigua was called at St. John's, to memorialize Parliament against the measure of abolition. When the meeting convened, the Hon. Samuel O. Baijer, who had been the champion of the opposition, was called upon to propose a plan of procedure. To the consternation of the pro-slavery meeting, their leader rose and spoke to the following effect: 'Gentlemen, my previous sentiments on this subject are well known to you all. Be not surprised to learn that they have undergone an entire change. I have not altered my views without deliberation. For several days past I have been making calculations with regard to the probable results of emancipation; and I have ascertained, beyond a doubt, that I can cultivate my estate at least one-third cheaper by free labor, than by slave labor.' The honorable gentleman proceeded to draw out the details of his calculations, and he presented an array of pecuniary considerations altogether new and imposing to the majority of the assembly. After he had finished his remarks, Mr. S. Shands, Member of Assembly, and a wealthy proprietor, observed that he entertained precisely the same views with those just expressed; but he thought the honorable gentleman had been unwise to utter them in so public a manner; for should these sentiments reach the ear of Parliament, it might induce them to withhold compensation. Colonel Edwards, Member of Assembly, rose and said he had long been opposed to slavery, but had not dared to avow his sentiments."

When the question came before the Colonial Assembly similar discussions ensued. The abolition of slavery was now seen to be inevitable. The only alternative presented to the colonists was the apprenticeship system, or immediate, unconditional emancipation. When the question came to this issue in the Antigua Assembly, both bodies *unanimously* passed a bill in favor of *immediate emancipation ;* on the ground that it was the wisest *policy.*

The first of August, 1834, was the day fixed by Parliament for the Abolition Act to go into effect. As the time approached, a heavy cloud lowered over the minds of most of the white population. A merchant of St. John's told Mr. Thome that several American vessels which had lain in the harbor, weighed anchor on the 31st of July, through actual fear that the island would be destroyed on the following day; and they earnestly entreated the merchant to escape with them, if he valued his life. Many planters believed it would be unsafe to go out in the evening, after emancipation. Some timid families did not venture to go to bed on the night of the 31st. They waited anxiously for the hour of midnight, fearing that the same bell which proclaimed "Liberty throughout the land, to *all* the inhabitants thereof," would prove the signal for general conflagration, and massacre of the white inhabitants.*

---

* There were in Antigua, at that time, 1,980 whites; 29,537 slaves; and 3,895 free colored people.

CHAPTER II.

ANTIGUA, AFTER IMMEDIATE, UNCONDITIONAL EMANCIPATION.

When the clock *began* to strike twelve, on the 31st of July, 1834, there were nearly 30,000 slaves in the island of Antigua; when it *ceased* to strike, they were all freemen!

I extract from Thome's West Indies the following account of that glorious transition: "The Wesleyans kept 'watch-night' in all their chapels. One of the missionaries gave us an account of the watch-meeting at the chapel in St. John's. The spacious house was filled with the candidates for liberty. All was animation and eagerness. A mighty chorus of voices swelled the song of expectation and joy; and, as they united in prayer, the voice of the leader was drowned in the universal acclamations of thanksgiving, and praise, and blessing, and honor, and glory to God, who had come down for their deliverance. In such exercises the evening was spent, until the hour of twelve approached. The missionary then proposed that when the cathedral clock should begin to strike, the whole congregation should fall on their knees, and receive the boon of freedom in silence. Accordingly, as the loud bell tolled its first note, the crowded assembly prostrated themselves. All was silence! save the quivering, half-stifled breath of the struggling spirit. Slowly the tones of the clock fell upon the waiting multitude. Peal on peal, peal on peal, rolled over the prostrate throng, like angels' voices, thrilling their weary heart-strings. Scarcely had the *last* tone sounded, when lightning flashed vividly, and a loud peal of thunder rolled through the sky. It was God's pillar of fire! His trump of Jubilee! It was followed by a moment of profound silence. Then came the outburst! They shouted 'Glory! Hallelujah!' They clapped their hands, they leaped up, they fell down, they clasped each other in their free arms, they cried, they laughed, they went to and fro, throwing upward their unfettered hands. High above all, a mighty sound ever and anon swelled up. It was the utterance of gratitude to God, in broken negro dialect.

"After this gush of excitement had spent itself, the congregation became calm, and religious exercises were resumed. The remainder of the night was spent in singing and prayer, in reading the Bible, and in addresses from the missionaries, explaining the nature of the freedom just received, and exhorting the people to be industrious, steady, and obedient to the laws, and to show themselves in all things worthy of the high boon God had conferred upon them.

"The first of August came on Friday; and a release from all work was proclaimed, until the next Monday. The great mass of the negroes spent the day chiefly in the churches and chapels. The clergy and missionaries, throughout the island, actively seized the opportunity to enlighten the people on all the duties and responsibilities of their new relation. We were assured that, in every quarter, the day was like a sabbath. A sabbath indeed! when 'the wicked ceased from troubling, and the weary were at rest.' Many of the planters informed us that they went to the chapels where their own people were assembled, and shook hands with them, and exchanged hearty good wishes.

"At Grace Hill, a Moravian missionary station, the emancipated negroes begged to have a sunrise meeting on the first of August, as they had been accustomed to have at Easter; and as it was the Easter Morning of their freedom, the request was granted. The people all dressed in white, and walked arm in arm to the chapel. There a hymn of thanksgiving was sung by the whole congregation kneeling. The singing was frequently interrupted by the tears and sobs of the melted people, until finally, they were overwhelmed by a tumult of emotion. The missionary, who was present, said the scene was indescribable.

"Planters and missionaries, in every part of the island, told us there was not a single dance, by night or day; not even so much as a fiddle played. There were no drunken carousals, no riotous assemblies. The emancipated were as far from dissipation and debauchery, as they were from violence and carnage. Gratitude was the absorbing emotion. From the hill-tops and the valleys, the cry of a disenthralled people went upward, like the sound of many waters: 'Glory to God! Glory to God!'

"Dr. Daniell, who has been long resident in Antigua, and has the management of several estates, told us that after such a prodigious change in the condition of the negroes, he expected some irregularities would ensue. He anticipated some relaxation from labor, during the week that followed emancipation. But on Monday morning, he found all his hands in the field; not one missing. The same day, he received a message from another estate, of which he was proprietor, that the negroes, to a man, had refused to go into the field. He immediately rode to the estate, and found the laborers, with hoes in their hands, doing nothing. Accosting them in a friendly manner, he inquired, 'What is the meaning of this? How is it that you are not at work this morning?' They immediately replied, 'It's not because we don't want to work, massa; but we wanted to see you, first and foremost, to know what the *bargain* would be.' As soon as that matter was settled, the whole body of negroes turned out cheerfully, without a moment's cavil. Mr Bourne, manager of Millar's estate, informed us that the largest gang he had ever seen in the field, on his property, turned out the week after the emancipation."

In the days of slavery, it had always been customary to order out the militia, during the Christmas holidays, when the negroes were in the habit of congregating in large numbers, to enjoy the festivities of the season. But the December after emancipation, the Governor issued a proclamation, that, "*in consequence of the abolition of slavery,*" there was no further need of taking that precaution. And it is a fact that there have been no soldiers out at Christmas, from that day to this. The Legislature of Antigua subsequently passed "an Act for the better organizing of the militia, the preamble of which reads thus: "Whereas *the abolition of slavery,* in this island, renders it expedient to provide against an *unnecessary augmentation* of the militia." etc. The public security and confidence were also strikingly indicated by the following military advertisement in 1836: "Recruits wanted! The freed men of Antigua are now called upon to show their gratitude to King William, for the benefits he has conferred on them and their families, by volunteering their services as soldiers in his First West India Regiment. By doing this, they will acquire a still higher rank in society, by being placed on a footing of perfect equality with the other troops in his majesty's service, and receive the same bounty, pay, clothing, rations, and allowances."

TESTIMONY OF PLANTERS IN ANTIGUA, IN 1837.

The Rev. James A. Thome, son of a slaveholder in Kentucky, visited the British West Indies in the autumn of 1836, and returned to this country in the summer of 1837. He published a book, soon after, from which I quote the following extracts:—

"We delivered a letter of introduction to Mr. James Howell, manager of Thibou Jarvis' estate. He told us that before emancipation took place, he had been strongly opposed to it; being exceedingly unwilling to give up his power of command. 'But,' said he, 'I shall never forget how differently I felt when freedom took place. I rose from my bed exclaiming, "I am free! I am free! I was the greatest slave on the estate; and now I am free."' He said that planters, who retained their harsh manner, did not succeed under the new system; but he never had any difficulty in managing his people. He found by experience that kindness and forbearance armed him with sufficient authority. The laborers on the estates he managed had been considerably reduced,* but the grounds had never been in a finer state of cultivation than at present. He said there would be a failure of crops, not from any fault of the laborers, but on account of a drought more prolonged, than he had known for thirty-six years. He said, 'When my work is backward, I give it out in jobs; and it is always done in half the usual time. Emancipation has almost wholly put an end to sulking, or pretending to be sick. That was a thing which

---

* This is accounted for, in many instances, by the women being withdrawn from field labor, to attend to their households; and by children being sent to school.

caused a vast deal of trouble during slavery. Every Monday morning, regularly, I used to find ten or a dozen round the door, waiting for my first appearance, to beg that they might be let off from work, on account of sickness. It was seldom that one-fourth of them were really unwell; but every one maintained he was sick; and, as it was hard to contend with them, they were sent off to the sick-house. Now, that is done away with. The hospitals on many estates are put to other uses. Mine is converted into a chapel. At first, the negroes showed some disposition to put on airs of independence; but that soon disappeared. They are always respectful in their manners. In that particular, there has been mutual improvement. Planters treat their laborers more like fellow-men, and that leads them to be respectful, in their turn. They have now a growing regard for character; a feeling unknown to them in the days of slavery. Their religious and moral condition was formerly very low, notwithstanding the efforts of the missionaries; but now it is rapidly improving.

"Mr. Armstrong, manager of Fitch's Creek estate, said to us: 'During slavery, I often used to lie sleepless in my bed, thinking of my dangerous situation; the only white person on the premises, far from help and surrounded by slaves. I have spent hours devising plans of defence, in case my house should be attacked by the negroes. I said to myself it would be useless to fire upon them. My only hope was to frighten the superstitious fellows, by covering myself with a white sheet, and rushing into the midst of them, like a ghost. But now I have the utmost confidence in my people. They have no *motive* now to prompt them to insurrection. They show great shrewdness in every thing that concerns their own interest. They are very exact in keeping their accounts with the manager. To a stranger, it must be incredible how they contrive to live on such small wages.' Mr. A. informed us that the spirit of enterprise, formerly dormant in Antigua, had been roused since emancipation. Planters were now beginning to inquire as to the best modes of cultivation, and to propose measures of general improvement. One of these measures was the establishment of Free Villages, in which the laborers from all the neighboring estates might dwell, by paying a small rent. Real estate has risen, and mercantile business greatly improved. Several missionaries were present while we talked with Mr. A.; and the whole company heartily joined in assuring us that a knowledge of the actual working of abolition in Antigua would be altogether favorable to the cause of freedom. They all agreed that the more thorough was our knowledge of the facts in the case, the more perfect would be our confidence in *immediate* emancipation.

"Dr. Ferguson, of St. John's called on us. He is a Member of Assembly, and one of the first physicians on the island. He said it had always appeared to him that if a man is peaceable while he is a slave, he would certainly be so when he was a freeman. But though he had anticipated beneficial results from the abolition of slavery, the reality had exceeded his most sanguine expectations. Had it not been for the unprecedented drought, the island would now be in a state of prosperity unequalled in any period of its history. The mercantile business of the town had increased astonishingly. He thought stores and shops had multiplied in a ratio of ten to one. Mechanical pursuits were likewise in a flourishing condition. A general spirit of enterprise was pervading the island. The streets and roads, in town and county, were much improved. The moral character of the white population was brightening; one proof of it was that the old custom of concubinage was becoming disreputable. Emancipation was working admirably ; especially for the planters. The credit of the island had decidedly improved. Immediate freedom was infinitely better policy than slavery, or the apprenticeship either.

"We visited Green Castle estate, about three miles from St. John's. The manager, Samuel Barnard Esq., received us kindly. He had been on the island forty-four years, engaged in the management of estates. He is now the owner of one estate, the manager of two, and attorney for six. He has grown old in the practice of slave-holding, and has survived the wreck of the system. Stripped of arbitrary power, he now lives among the freed people, who were once his slaves, in the house where his grandfather was murdered in his bed by his slaves. The testimony of such a man is invaluable. He said the transition from slavery to freedom was like passing suddenly out of a dark dungeon into the sunlight.

2*

He thought the Assembly had acted wisely in adopting *immediate* emancipation. The endless altercations and troubles of the apprenticeship system had thus been avoided. The negroes made no riot or disturbance when they received their freedom; and he had no difficulty about their working. Some estates had suffered for a short time. There was a pretty general fluctuation, for a month or two, owing to the laborers leaving one estate and going to another; but that was because the planters overbid each other, to get the best hands. The negroes had a very strong attachment to their homes, and would rarely leave them, unless harshly treated. Very few of his people had left him. There were some inconveniences connected with the present system, but they were incomparably less than those connected with slavery.

"Dr. Daniell, manager of the Weatherill estate, has long been a resident of Antigua, and is thoroughly acquainted with its internal policy. He is a Member of the Council, owns an estate, manages another, and is attorney for six. Being a prominent member of one branch of the body which gave immediate emancipation to the slaves, his testimony is entitled to great weight. He said, 'We all violently resisted abolition, when it began to be agitated in England. We regarded it as an outrageous interference with our property and our rights. But now we are rejoiced that slavery is abolished.' He did not think the system of apprenticeship had any tendency to prepare the slaves for freedom. The arbitrary control of a master could never be a preparation for freedom. Sound, wholesome legal restraints were the only preparation. Apprenticeship vexed and harrassed the negroes, and kept them in a state of suspense. The reflection that they had been cheated out of their expected liberty six years would sour their minds; and when they at last obtained freedom, they would be less likely to be grateful. The planters in Antigua had secured the attachment of their people by conferring upon them immediate emancipation. There had been no deficiency of labor. Estates throughout the island were never in more advanced condition. Nothing was wanted but rain. He frequently employed his people by the job, for short periods, and always with gratifying results. The negroes accomplished twice as much as when they worked for daily wages, because they made more money.

On some days they made three shillings; three times the ordinary wages. He managed them altogether by mildness, and found it extremely easy. He had quite as much influence over them, as he ever had during slavery. But where managers persisted in habits of arbitrary command, they failed. He had been obliged to discharge a manager from one of his estates, on account of his overbearing disposition. If he had not dismissed him, the people would have abandoned the estate. Love of home was such a passion with negroes, that nothing but bad treatment could force them away. He did not know of more than one or two planters on the whole island, who did not consider emancipation a decided advantage to all parties.

"Dr. Nugent, manager of Lyon's estate, has long been Speaker of the Assembly, and is favorably known in Europe as a man of science. No man in Antigua stands higher. He owns one estate and manages another. He told us that, previous to emancipation, no man dared to express opposition to slavery, if he wished to maintain a respectable standing. Planters might have their hopes but they could not make them public, without incurring general odium, and being denounced as enemies of their country. The most general prediction was that the negroes would not work after they were free; but time had proved there was no foundation for that apprehension. The estates were never in better order than at present. On account of the stimulus of wages, there was far less feigned sickness, than during slavery. The sick-house used to be thronged with real or pretended invalids; now the negroes don't go near it. The one on his estate was now used for a stable. He thought the capabilities of the blacks for education and for trades, were conspicuous. Emancipation had proved a blessing to the masters, and as for the advantages to the slave, they were too obvious to need to be pointed out. Insurrection or revenge was in no case dreaded; not even by those planters who had been most cruel. After slavery was abolished, there remained no *motive* for rebellion. The expenses of cultivation were greatly diminished, and machinery and cattle more generally used than formerly.

"Mr. Hatly, manager of Frey's estate, told us the improved industry and efficiency of his people had encouraged him to bring several additional acres under cultivation. They did not require such constant watching as formerly. They took much more interest in the prosperity of the estate, than they did when they were slaves. He showed us his accounts for the last year of slavery, and the first year of freedom; they proved a reduction of expenses more than one-third. He said, 'The old habit of feigning sickness is broken up. During slavery, this was more or less the case every week, sometimes every day, and it was exceedingly annoying. One would come, carrying his arm on his hand, declaring it had such a mighty pain in it, he couldn't use the hoe no way; another would make his appearance with both hands on his breast, and, with a rueful look, complain of a great pain in his stomach; a third came limping along, with a dreadful *rheumatis* in his knees; and so on, for a dozen or more. It was in vain to dispute with them, though it was often manifest that nothing on earth ailed them. They would say, "Ah, me, massa, you no tink how bad me feel. It's deep *in*, massa." But we have no feigned sickness now, and much less actual illness than formerly. My people now say they have no time to be sick. We formerly had strong prejudices against the plough; but now it is beginning to be extensively used, and we find it greatly reduces the necessary amount of labor. I have already seen such decided benefits growing out of the free labor system, that I never wish to see the face of slavery again. We are relieved from the painful task of flogging. Formerly, it was nothing but whip, whip, whip. Now we know no more of the lash.'

"David Cranstoun, Esq., manager of Athill's estate, and a magistrate, said to us: 'I get my work done better than formerly, and with incomparably more cheerfulness. I employ fewer laborers, but my estate was never in a finer state of cultivation. My people are always ready and willing to work. I occasionally employ them at jobs, and always with great success. When I give out a job, it is accomplished in half the time it would have taken, if paid by the day. On such occasions, I have known them turn out before three o'clock in the morning, and work by moonlight: and when the moon was not shining, they sometimes kindled fires among the dry cane leaves to work by. They would continue working all day, till four o'clock; stopping only for breakfast, and dispensing with the usual intermission from twelve to two. During slavery, the weekly expenses on the estate averaged £45 ($218.02). After emancipation, they averaged £20 ($96.90). The negroes are a remarkably temperate people. I have rarely seen one intoxicated. We have no cause to fear insurrections now. Emancipation has freed us from all danger on that score. Among the advantages of the present system is the greater facility of managing estates. It saves us from a world of trouble and perplexity. I have found that the negroes are easily controlled by law; more so, perhaps, than the laboring classes in other countries. I do not know of a single planter, who would be willing to have slavery restored. We feel that it was a great curse; a curse to the planter, as well as the slave.'

"We breakfasted at the Villa estate, within half a mile of St. John's. We found the manager less sanguine in his views of emancipation, than the planters generally were. This is easily accounted for. The estate is situated so near the seaport town, that his people have many temptations to leave their work, from which those on more distant estates are exempt. He admitted, however, that the danger of insurrection was removed, that crime was lessened, and the moral condition of society rapidly improving.

"Mr. Bourne, manager of Millar's estate, said : ' Fearing the consequences of emancipation, I reduced my cultivation in 1831; but soon finding that my people would work as well as ever, I brought it up to the customary extent, the next year; and this year, I have added fifteen acres of new land. I have no hesitation in saying that, if I have a supply of cash, I can take off any crop it may please God to send. Nothing but bad treatment ever makes the negroes leave estates on which they have been accustomed to live; and in such cases, a change of management has almost uniformly proved sufficient to induce them to return. They are decidedly less prone to be insolent now, than during slavery. The expense of managing estates has diminished one-third. Before emancipation, very little was thought about expedients for saving manual labor; but many improvements have already been introduced, and more are suggested. Emancipation has proved an incalculable blessing to the planters, by releasing them from an endless complication of responsibilities, perplexities, temptations, and anxieties; especially, because it has relieved them from the bondage of the whip. It was hard work to be a Christian in the days of slavery. Yes, I assure you, sir, it was *very* hard to be a Christian in those days.'

"Ralph Higinbotham, Esq., U. S. Consul at Antigua, in 1837, bore the following testimony: 'The general conduct of the negroes has been worthy of much praise; especially considering the sudden transition from slavery to unrestricted freedom. Their demeanor is peaceable and orderly. Whatever may have been the dissatisfaction of the planters at the commencement of the present system, they are now well satisfied that their properties are better worked, and their laborers more contented and cheerful, than in the time of slavery.'"

Some difficulties always attend every change in the structure of society; but if the change is based on true principles, the difficulties are always temporary. They are like a stony pathway from a cavern into sunlight. So it proved in Antigua. Mr. James Scotland, the venerable merchant already alluded to, said to Mr. Thome: "The troubles attending emancipation resulted almost entirely from the perseverance of the planters in their old habits of dominion. Their pride was wounded by seeing their slaves elevated to equal rights, and they were jealous lest they should aspire to be on the same footing in all respects. In the early stage of freedom, they frequently used their power as employers to the annoyance and injury of their laborers. For the slightest misconduct, and sometimes without any reason whatever, the poor negroes were dragged before magistrates (who were planters, or the friends of planters), mulcted in their wages, fined otherwise, and committed to jail, or the house of correction. Yet those harrassed people remained patient, orderly, and submissive. Their treatment has now much improved; for the planters have happily discovered that they sacrificed their own interests by keeping the cultivators of their lands in agitation and suffering."

TESTIMONY OF MAGISTRATES AND TEACHERS, IN ANTIGUA, IN 1837.

Mr. Thome says: "The governor spoke to us unreservedly of the past and present condition of Antigua, and stated various particulars in which the Colony had been greatly improved by emancipation. He said planters from every part of the island assured him that the negroes were industriously disposed. They all conceded that emancipation had proved a blessing to the island, and he did not know a single individual who wished to return to the old system. He said that, during the recent Christmas holidays, the Police Reports did not return a single case of arrest. He had been acquainted with the country districts in England, and travelled extensively in Europe; and he had never yet found such a peaceable, orderly, law-abiding peasantry, as those of Antigua. The great crime of the island, and indeed, of all the West India Colonies, had been licentiousness; but they were certainly fast improving in that particular.

"By invitation of the Governor, we attended him to the annual examination of the parochial school in St. John's. He requested that all the children emancipated on the first of August, 1834, might be called up. It was a most interesting and beautiful sight. Nearly one hundred children, from black to the clearest white, who two years ago were slaves, stood there before us free. When we spoke to them of emancipation, their animated looks and gestures, and their lively tones in answering our questions, showed that they felt it was a blessing to be free. There was as much respectfulness, attention, and general intelligence, as we ever saw in scholars of the same age. His Excellency expressed himself highly pleased with the appearance and proficiency of the school. Turning to us, he said, in a tone of pleasantry, 'You see, gentlemen, these children have *souls*.'

"Teachers, missionaries, clergymen, and planters, uniformly testified that the negroes were as capable of receiving instruction as any people in the world; and it was confirmed beyond all doubt by facts we ourselves witnessed. We were happy to learn that the emancipated negroes manifested great anxiety for the education of their children. They encouraged them to go to school, and labored to support them, though they had strong temptation to detain them at home to work. They also contributed a small weekly sum for the maintenance of schools."

Concerning the moral condition of Antigua, Mr. Thome furnishes a quantity of Police Reports, from which I quote the following, as fair samples of the whole: " St. John's, Sept. 1835. Capital offences have much decreased in number, as well as all minor ones. The principal crimes lately submitted for the investigation of the magistrates seem to consist chiefly in trifling offences, and breaches of contract.

" Oct. 1835. Although instances do occur of breaches of contract, they are not very frequent; and, in many cases, I have been induced to believe that the offence has originated more in want of a proper understanding of the time, intent, and meaning of the contract into which the laborers have entered, than from the actual existence of any dissatisfaction on their part.

"Jan. 1836. (Immediately after the Christmas holidays.) At this period, when several successive days of idleness occur among the laboring classes, I cannot but congratulate your Honor on the quiet demeanor and general good order, which has happily been maintained throughout the island. During the holidays I had only one prisoner committed to my charge, and his offence was of a minor nature.

" Feb. 1836. I beg leave to congratulate your Honor on the vast diminution of all minor misdemeanors, and the total absence of capital offences.

" Sept. 1836. The agricultural laborers continue a steady and uniform line of conduct, and, with some few exceptions, afford general satisfaction to their employers. Every friend to this country, and to the liberties of the world, must view with satisfaction the gradual improvement in the character and behavior of this class of the community, under the constant operation of the local enactments.

" Jan. 1837. (After the Christmas holidays.) I cordially congratulate your Excellency on the regular and steady behavior maintained by all ranks of society, at this particular season of the year. Not one crime of a heinous nature has been discovered. I proudly venture to declare my opinion that in no part of his Majesty's dominions has a pupulation of 30,000 conducted themselves with more strict propriety, at this annual festival, or been more peaceably obedient to the laws.

"Feb. 1837. Crimes of any heinous nature are very rare among the laborers. I may venture to say that petty thefts, breaking sugar canes to eat, and offences of the like description, principally swell the calendars of our Quarterly Courts of Sessions. In general, the laborers are peaceable, orderly, and civil; not only to those who move in higher spheres of life, but also to each other."

The foregoing Reports are all signed by "Richard S. Wickham, Superintendent of Police."

TESTIMONY OF CLERGY AND MISSIONARIES IN ANTIGUA, IN 1837.

Rev. Mr. Jones, Rector of St. Phillips, said to Mr. Thome:—"The planters have always been opposed to improvements, until they were effected, and the good results became manifest. They first said that the abolition of the slave-*trade* would ruin the Colonies; next they said the abolition of *slavery* would be the certain destruction of the islands; and now they deprecate the *education* of the emancipated children, as a measure fraught with disastrous consequences. But emancipation has proved a great blessing to the people, and the planters in this part of the island are gratified with the working of the system. The benefits of education are extending, and religious privileges greatly increasing. There has been manifest improvement in the morals and manners of the children, since education has become general. With regard to marriage, there has been a complete revolution in the habits of the people.

"The Superintendent of the Wesleyan Mission informed us that the collection in the several Wesleyan Chapels, in 1836, independent of occasional contributions to Sunday Schools, missionary objects, etc., amounted to more than $6,000. Besides giving liberally, according to their small means, to the Bible Society, the emancipated slaves formed several Branch Associations among themselves, for the circulation of the Scriptures. The contributions from Antigua and Bermuda, the only two islands which had then adopted *entire* freedom, were *double* those from any other two islands.

Among the Wesleyans, the freed negroes had formed four Friendly Societies, to help the aged and infirm, nurse the sick, and encourage sobriety and industry. In 1836, they raised money themselves and expended for those objects £700 currency ($2,100). In 1837, they had £600 ($1.800) in their treasury." To estimate this liberality properly, it must be remembered that the wages of these poor people was only a shilling a day, about twenty-four cents: and that they boarded themselves; also, that, until the last three years, they had received no wages at all for their labor. There was no public poorhouse in Antigua; a fact highly creditable to the emancipated people.

A Report published by the Wesleyan Brethren, alluding to the emancipated slaves, says: "They always show a readiness to contribute to the support of the Gospel. With the present low wages, and the entire charge of self-maintenance, they have but little to spare. Parham and Sion Hill (taken as specimens) have societies composed almost entirely of rural blacks; about 1,350 in number. In 1836, these contributed above $1,650, in little weekly subscriptions; besides giving to special objects occasionally, and contributing for the support of schools."

The West India Association for Advancement of Christian Faith, in its Report for 1836, makes a statement which shows that marriages in *one* year, at that time, were *twice* as numerous as in *ten* years, during slavery.

TESTIMONY OF THE EMANCIPATED SLAVES IN ANTIGUA, IN 1837.

Mr. Thome says: "A young negro, who had been a slave, rowed us across the harbor of St. John's. We asked him about the first of August, 1834. He said: 'Dar was more religious on dat day, dan you can tink of.' When we questioned him about the laws, he said the law was his friend. If there was no law to take his part, a strong man might knock him down; but now everybody feared the law. The masters *would* sometimes slash a fellow, let him do his *best;* but the law never hurt anybody that behaved well.

"We asked an old negro what he did on the first of August. He replied: 'Massa, we went to church, and tank de Lord for make a we all free.'

"We asked two men, who were masons on an estate, how they liked liberty. They replied: 'O sir, it is very comfortable; very comfortable indeed. The day when freedom come, we was as happy as though we was just going to Heaven. We used to think very much about being free; but we did not hope it would ever be, till death delivered us from bondage. Now we've got free, we wouldn't sell ourselves for any money. The money would soon be gone; but freedom will last as long as we live.' We asked if they wouldn't be willing to sell themselves to a man they were sure would treat them well. They immediately replied: 'We should be willing to *serve* such a man; but we wouldn't *sell* ourselves to the best man in the world.' They said they were very desirous to have their children learn all they could, while they were young; for education was a great thing.

"On our way to Grace Bay, we met some negro men at work on the road, and stopped to chat with them. We asked them if they danced on the first of August. They quickly replied, 'Oh! oh! no fiddling *den!* No, me massa. All go to church *dat* day.' One of them said, 'I always thought much about freedom, but I no hope eber to be free. One morning, bout four o'clock, I was walking along de road, all lone, and I prayed dat de Saviour would make me free; for den I could be *so* happy! I don't know what made me pray so; for I wasn't looking for de free; but in one month de free come.' They told us they worked a great deal better, since they were paid for it. I asked one of them whether he wouldn't be willing to be a slave again, if he could always be sure of a good master. He exclaimed: 'Heigh! me massa! Me nebber be slave, no more! A good massa a bery good ting; but freedom till better.' They told us it was a great blessing to have their children go to school.

"An intelligent colored gentleman informed us that while the negroes were slaves, they used to spend, during the Christmas holidays, all the money they got during the year; but now they saved it carefully, to buy small tracts of land for their own cultivation."

At the examination of one of the schools, several women who worked on the estates, who had children in the school, put on their Sunday's best, and went to hear the classes recite. When Mr. Thome spoke to one of them about the privileges her children enjoyed, her eyes filled with tears, and she replied, "Yes, massa, we do tank de good Lord for bring de free. Never can be too tankful." She said she had seven children present, and it made her feel happy to have them learn to read. Another said, when she heard the children reading so well, she wanted "to take de words out of da mouts, and put 'em in her own." She added, "I tell you, massa, it do my old heart good to come here."

"Old Grandfather Jacob, who had been a deacon in one of the Moravian churches, told us of the dungeons in which the slaves used to be confined; and with much feeling, said his wife had once been put into a damp dungeon. Some got sick there, and were never well afterward. He knew one that died there. He had been flogged twice for leaving his work to bury the dead. 'Can't put we in dungeon *now!*' exclaimed Grandfather Jacob, with a triumphant look. 'No lick we! If dey no like we, tell we to go away; dat's all.' We asked if he was provided for by the manager. He said no, his children supported him. 'Now, when ole man die, him children make coffin, and put him in de ground!' We asked whether it was not better for an old man to be a slave, so as to get food and clothing from the manager. He darted a quick look at us, and said, 'Radder be free.'

"Mr. and Mrs. Möhne, Moravian missionaries, told us that, though the low rate of wages was scarcely sufficient to support life, they had never seen a single individual, who desired to be a slave again. Even the aged and infirm, who sometimes suffered, from neglect of the planters, and the inability of their relatives to provide adequately for them, expressed the liveliest gratitude for the great blessing the Lord had given them. They would often say, 'Missus, ole sinner just sinkin in de grave; but de good Lord let me ole eyes see dis blessed sun.'"

CHAPTER III.

THE WINDWARD ISLANDS, DURING THE APPRENTICE-
SHIP—TESTIMONY OF PLANTERS IN BARBADOES, IN
1837.*

Mr. Thome says: "Soon after we arrived in Barbadoes we visited Mr. C., manager of Lear's estate, about four miles from Bridgetown. He had been a planter for thirty-six years. He was attorney for two other large estates, and had under his superintendence more than a thousand apprenticed laborers. He said, 'I often wished that slavery might be abolished, and other planters of my acquaintance had the same feelings; but we did not dare to express them. Most of the planters were so violently opposed to emancipation, that even up to the 31st of July, they declared it could not and should not take place. Now, these very men see and acknowledge the benefits which are resulting from the new system. Slavery was a reign of terror. I have often started up from a dream in which I thought my room was filled with armed slaves. But all such fears have passed away. There is no *motive* for insurrection now. On the first of August, 1834, the people labored on the estates the same as usual. If a stranger had gone over the island, he would not have suspected that any change had taken place. I told my people, the day before, that under the new laws they were to turn out at six o'clock in the morning, instead of at five, as formerly. I did not expect they would go to work that day; but, at the appointed hour, they were all in the field; not one was missing. They do more work in the nine hours required by present laws, than they did in the twelve hours, exacted under slavery. They are more faithful, than when they were slaves. They take more interest

---

* The population of Barbadoes was 14,959 whites; 82,807 slaves; 5,146 free colored people.

in the prosperity of the estate, and in seeing that things are not destroyed. There is less theft, because they begin to have some respect for character. They can now appeal to the law for protection; and their respect for law is very great. They are always willing to work for me during their own time, for which I pay them twenty-five cents a day. I have planted thirty additional acres this year, and have taken a larger crop than I have ever taken. The island has never been under such good cultivation, and it is becoming better every year. Real estate has increased in value more than thirty per cent. Emancipation was a great blessing, to the master, as well as the slave. It was emancipation to *me*. You cannot imagine the responsibilities and anxieties that were swept away with the extinction of slavery. There are many annoying circumstances connected with slavery, which have a pernicious effect on the master. There is continual jealousy and suspicion between him and his slaves. They look upon each other as natural enemies. A perpetual system of plotting and counter-plotting is kept up. Flogging was a matter of course throughout the island, while slavery existed. It was as common to strike a slave, as to strike a horse. Very often, it was merely because the master happened to be in an irritable mood, and the slave had no idea what he was punished for. I have myself, more than once, ordered slaves to be flogged, when I was in a passion, and after I was cool I would have given guineas not to have done it. I believe emancipation will save the souls of many planters. If it is hard for a rich man to enter the kingdom of heaven, it is much harder for a planter. I sometimes wonder at myself, when I think how long I was connected with slavery; but self-interest and custom blinded me to its enormities. I lately met with a planter, who, up to the last of July, had maintained that the mother country could not be so mad as to take a step that would inevitably ruin her Colonies. Now, he would be the last man to vote for the restoration of slavery. He even wants to get rid of the apprenticeship, and adopt immediate, unconditional emancipation, as they did in Antigua. Such changes of opinion are very common among the planters. I think the expenses under apprenticeship are about the same as during slavery; but calculations I have made convince me that under an entirely free system, I could cultivate this estate for $3,000 a year less than it formerly cost. I have no doubt the negroes will work, when their freedom comes in 1840. There may be a little excited, experimenting feeling, for a short time, but I am confident that things generally will move on peaceably and prosperously. The slaves were well acquainted with the efforts made in England for their emancipation. They used to watch the arrival of every packet with extreme anxiety. If Parliament had refused to abolish slavery, there would have been a general insurrection. While there was hope, they waited peaceably for release; but if hope had been destroyed, slavery would have been buried in blood. The apprenticeship caused some dissatisfaction among them. They thought they ought to be entirely free, and they suspected that their masters were deceiving them. At first, they could not understand the conditions of the new system; and there was some murmuring among them; but they concluded it was better to wait six years more for the desired boon, than to lose it by revolt.'

"Samuel Hinkston, Esq., manager of Colliton estate, and one of the local magistrates, gave an account similar in all respects, to that given by the manager of Lear's. He had been a planter for thirty-six years, and was universally esteemed for his humane character, and close attention to business. He said his apprentices never refused to work in the hours required by law, and during their own time, they were always ready to work for him, for wages, whenever he needed them. When he had no occasion for them, they often let themselves out to work on other people's grounds. Real estate had risen very much, and it was universally conceded that the island had never been under better cultivation. In every respect, the new system worked better than the old; but he looked forward with pleasure to the still better change that would come in 1840. He believed unconditional freedom would remove all annoyances. His only regret was that it could not come sooner.

"We were invited to visit Col. Ashby; an aged and experienced planter, who resides in the southernmost part of the island. He told us he had been a practical planter ever since 1795. He had violently opposed abolition, and regarded the anti-slavery members of Parliament with unmingled hatred. He thought no punishment, either in this life, or the life to come, was too bad for Wilberforce. When he told us this, he exclaimed, ' But, oh, how mistaken I was about that man! I am convinced of it now. The abolition of slavery has proved an incalculable blessing.' He dwelt much on the trustiness and strong attachment of the negroes, when they were well treated. They were never disposed to leave their employer, unless he was intolerably passionate and hard with them. He said he avoided, as much as possible, carrying his apprentices before a special magistrate; and he always found it easy to settle difficulties himself by a conciliatory course."

Mr. Thome was introduced to one planter, whose name he does not mention, probably because his neighbors gave him the character of having been a cruel master, during slavery. He retained the prejudices natural to that class of men. "He complained that the negroes were an ungrateful, perverse set; the more they were indulged, the more lazy and insolent they became. He said he knew that by his *own* experience. One fault he had to find with all his apprentices, both in the house and in the field; they all held him to the letter of the *law*, and were always ready to arraign him before a special magistrate for any infraction of it. He also considered it a great grievance that women with young babies were unwilling to work in the field, as they did formerly; now 'they spent half their time taking care of their brats.' He however acknowledged that his apprentices were willing to work, that his estates were never under better cultivation, and that he could say the same for estates all over the island."

Dr. Bell, a planter from Demerara, was on a visit to Barbadoes, and Mr. Thome made some inquiries concerning the results of abolition there. "He said the Colony was now suffering for want of laborers; but after the apprentices were free, in 1840, there would doubtless be increased emigration thither, from older and less productive Colonies. The planters were making arrangements for cultivating sugar on a larger scale than ever before, and estates were selling at very high prices. Every thing indicated the fullest confidence that the prosperity of the country would be permanent and progressive."

Mr. Thome says: "We had repeated interviews with gentlemen, who were well acquainted with the adjacent islands; one of them was proprietor of a sugar estate in St. Vincent's. They all assured us that in those islands there reigned the same tranquillity that we saw in Barbadoes. Sir Evan McGregor, Governor-General of all the Windward Colonies, and of course thoroughly informed respecting their internal condition, gave us the same assurances. From these authentic sources, we learned enough to satisfy ourselves, that in all the Colonies, conciliatory and equitable management has never failed to secure peace and industry."

TESTIMONY OF MAGISTRATES IN BARBADOES, IN 1837.

Mr. Thome says: "The Governor, Sir Evan McGregor, told us he had been five years in the West Indies, and had resided at Antigua and Dominica before he received his present appointment; he had also visited several other islands. He said that in no place he had visited had things gone on so quietly and satisfactorily, to all classes, as in Antigua. The apprenticeship system was vexatious to both parties. It kept up a constant state of warfare between master and apprentice, and engendered bitter feeling on both sides. To some extent, that was the case in Barbadoes; but it would doubtless pass away with the present impolitic system. He was so well satisfied that unconditional freedom was better, both for the masters and the laborers, that, if he had the power, he would emancipate every apprentice to-morrow.

"Hon. R. B. Clarke, Solicitor General, candidly owned that while abolition was pending in Parliament, he had declared, publicly and repeatedly that it would ruin the Colonies; but the results had proved so different, that he was ashamed of his forebodings. He said there were many fears about the first of August. He rose early that morning, and rode twelve miles over the most populous part of the island; and when he saw all the negroes peaceably at their work, he felt satisfied that all would go well."

Major Colthurst, Special Magistrate, gave a written testimony to Mr. Thome, from which I extract the following: "The number of apprenticed laborers in my district, is 9,480. In consequence of its vicinity to the large seaport of Bridgetown, it is perhaps the most troublesome district in the island. In the more rural districts, not above half as many complaints are made to the magistrates. There has been no trouble in my district, occasioned by the apprentices refusing to work. They work manfully and cheerfully, wherever they are treated with humanity and consideration. I have never known an instance to the contrary. When the conductor of the estate is wanting in this respect, disinclination to perform their duties is the natural consequence; but the interference of the magistrate soon sets matters right. The number of complaints brought before me are much fewer than last year, and their character is also greatly improved. Nine complaints out of ten are for small impertinences and saucy answers; which, considering the former and present condition of the parties, is naturally to be expected; but the number even of such complaints is much diminished. It is amazing how few material breaches of the law occur in so extraordinary a community. Occasionally, there are a few cases of crime; but when it is considered that the population of this island is nearly as dense as that of any part of China, and wholly uneducated, either by precept or example, this absence of frequent crime excites our wonder, and is highly creditable to the negroes. I do not hesitate to say that perfect tranquillity exists in this Colony, though passing through one of the most momentous changes, that ever took place in any age, or country; the passage of nearly 80,000 slaves from bondage to freedom. The apprentices are inclined to purchase their discharge; especially when misunderstandings occur with their masters. When they obtain it, they generally labor in the trades and occupations, to which they were previously accustomed, and conduct themselves well. They seldom take to drinking. Indeed, the black and colored population are the most temperate people I ever knew. The experience of nearly forty years, in various public situations, confirms me in this very important fact."

Testimony similar to the above is adduced from a number

of magistrates and police officers. They all agreed that vice and crime had diminished, and were disminishing; that the feeling of security was universal; that land was rising; and that even the most prejudiced planters would not return to the old system, if they could.

TESTIMONY OF CLERGY AND MISSIONARIES IN BARBADOES, IN 1837.

Mr. Thome says: "Rev. Edward Elliott, the Archdeacon at Barbadoes, informed us that the number of clergymen and churches had increased since emancipation; religious meetings were more fully attended, and the instructions given manifestly had greater influence. Increased attention was paid to education also. The clergy, and the Moravian and Wesleyan Missionaries had put forth new efforts, and were opening schools in various parts of the island. Before emancipation, the planters opposed education, and, as far as possible, prevented teachers from coming on their estates. Now, they encouraged it in many instances, and where they did not directly encourage it, they made no opposition. He said the number of marriages had very much increased. He was convinced that no bad results would have followed, if entire freedom had been granted in 1834, as in Antigua. While slavery continued, people did fear insurrections; but he did not think five planters on the island had any fear now.

"Rev. Mr. Fidler, Superintendent of the Wesleyan Missions, told us the Methodists had been violently persecuted in Barbadoes, during the reign of slavery. Their chapel in Bridgetown had been utterly demolished by a mob, and some of the missionaries obliged to fly for their lives. But things had very much altered since emancipation. Several estates were now open to the missionaries, and churches were being built in various parts of the country. One man, who helped to pull down the chapel, had now given land to build a new one; and had offered the free use of one of his buildings, for religious meetings, and a school, until it could be erected.

"Rev. Mr. Cummins, Curate of St. Paul's, in Bridgetown, told us his sabbath school had greatly increased since emancipation. The negroes manifested an increasing desire for religious instruction, and he was convinced they had as much capacity for learning, as the whites. All the churches were now crowded, and there was an increasing demand for more. Their morals had greatly improved; especially with respect to marriage.

"We visited an infant school, connected with the Episcopal church, established two weeks previous, for the children of the apprenticed laborers. The teacher, who has been for many years an instructor, told us he found them as quick to learn, as any children he ever taught. He had been surprised to see how soon the instructions of the schoolroom were carried home to the parents. The very first night, after the school closed, he heard the children repeating what they had been taught, and the parents learning the songs from their lips.

"Rev. Mr. Walton, from Montserrat, told us the planters on that island were getting tired of the apprenticeship, and, from mere considerations of interest and comfort, were adopting free labor. There had been repeated instances of planters emancipating all their apprentices. He said a new impulse had been given to education. Schools were springing up in all parts of the island. Marriages were occurring every week. The planters now encouraged missionaries to labor among their people, and were ready to give land for chapels, which were fast multiplying."

NEGRO TESTIMONY IN BARBADOES, IN 1837.

Mr. Thome says: "The tender of the sugar-mill at Lear's was an old negro, with furrowed brow and thin gray locks. We asked him how they were getting along under the new system. He replied, 'Bery well, massa, tank God. All peaceable and good.' 'Then you like apprenticeship better than slavery?' 'Great deal better, massa. We'se doing well, now.' 'You like apprenticeship as well as freedom, don't you?' 'Oh, no, me massa. Freedom till better.' 'What would you do, if you were entirely free?' 'We mus work, massa. All hab to work, when de free come.

'How are you treated now?' 'Bery well, tank God.' No flogging, no shutting up in dungeon, now.' 'But what makes you want freedom? You are so old, you couldn't enjoy it long.' 'Me want to *die* free, massa. It good ting to die free. And me want to see children free, too.'"

CHAPTER IV.

TESTIMONY CONCERNING THE WEST INDIES, FROM 1840 TO 1859.

Joseph J. Gurney, of England, visited the British West Indies in 1840. At St. Christopher's, the Solicitor General of the Colony told him that a small estate on the island sold shortly before emancipation, with all the slaves on it, for £2,000. He said, six years afterward, it would sell, without the slaves for £6,000. Mr. Gurney adds: "This remarkable rise in the value of property is by no means confined to particular estates." "In this island, the negroes perform a far greater amount of work in a given time, than could be obtained from them under slavery. One of my informants said, 'They will do an infinity of work for wages.'"

Sir William Colebrook, Governor of Antigua, and Mr. Gilbert, a clergyman, both gave the following testimony to Mr. Gurney: "At the lowest computation, the land, without a single slave upon it, is fully as valuable now, as it was, including all the slaves, before emancipation." Mr. Gilbert told Mr. Gurney that the compensation he received for his slaves, from the British government, was "a mere present put into his pocket; a gratuity, on which he had no reasonable claim. For his land, *without* the slaves, was at least of the same value that it formerly was *with* the slaves; and since emancipation, his profits had increased."

At Dominica, Mr. Gurney found the emancipated laborers "working cheerfully, and cheaply to their employers, as compared with slavery."

Concerning the islands he visited, Mr. Gurney says: "The change for the better, in the dress, demeanor, and welfare of the people, is prodigious. The imports are vastly increased. The duties on imports in St. Christopher's were £1,000 more in 1838 than they were in 1837; and in 1839, they were double what they were in 1838, within £150. This surprising increase is owing to the demand, on the part of the freed laborers for imported goods; especially for articles of dress."

In May, 1846, Dr. John Davy, author of a work on the West Indies, and brother of the celebrated Sir Humphrey Davy, wrote from Barbadoes, where he was residing, in official and professional employment, to the well-known Mr. George Combe, of Edinburgh. The letter was published in *The Liberty Bell*, for 1847, and I make the following extracts from it:—

"I could wish that those who still approve of slavery, or who may consider it a necessary evil, would pay a visit to the West Indies, especially to this island, and witness the effects of emancipation. I am much mistaken if they would not go back satisfied that the abolition of slavery has here been, in every respect, advantageous; to the negroes, to the planters, and to the population generally. I have been in Barbadoes very nearly a year, and I have conversed on the subject with proprietors of estates, who formerly owned slaves, with merchants, and with colored people, who had been slaves. Among them all, there seemed to be but one feeling; that emancipation was a blessing, and that were it possible to bring back slavery, all would be opposed to it.

"When slavery existed, there was always fear of insurrection, especially in times of danger, whether connected with war, or other calamities, such as fires and hurricanes. Then, it was necessary to have a standing militia, always ready to act. It was necessary to have beacons and forts, to give the alarm and afford defence. Now, there is a perfect feeling of security. The population is considered as one; bound together by common rights and common interests. The militia has been disbanded, and is not likely to be re-organized, except on a threatening of war. Forts are no longer required. Some of them have been dismantled and are forgotten. Some are converted into stations for the police; a body chiefly composed of colored men. Prior to abolition, from what I can learn, crime of every kind was more prevalent; especially robbery. Then, there was always at large a certain number of runaway slaves, who supported themselves by nightly depredations, and, occasionally collecting into large parties, broke into and plundered the houses of the opulent. Since the abolition of slavery, I have not heard of the murder of a white man, nor of any instance of revenge taken by the liberated for cruel treatment inflicted before liberation. I have not heard of any instances of house breaking, or of robbery, except of a petty kind, commonly designated as pilfering. The security, as to property, in which the opulent live here is remarkable. But it is not surprising, when we reflect on the easy condition of the people generally. Want is almost unknown, beggars are almost unknown; yet there are no poor laws, and no provision made by law for the support of paupers.

"The freed laborers are contented with a shilling sterling (twenty-four cents) a day for their work, men and women alike. This is sufficient to supply their wants, and to enable them to have some comforts, and even luxuries, where the ordinary articles of diet are cheap, and where most laborers have a portion of land, for which they pay rent. Commonly, on every estate requiring over a hundred laborers, there is a village, where those who work on the estate reside. To be near their work is an advantage to both laborers and proprietors; and it being for the interest of the latter to attach the former to them, they are dealt with kindly and liberally. If other treatment is experienced, the laborers seek employment elsewhere, and have no difficulty in finding it. This, it must be admitted, is a happy change, and worth some pecuniary sacrifices; but it is doubtful whether it entailed any such. I have been assured by many managers of estates, well acquainted with the minute details of expenditure under the former and the present systems of slave labor and free labor, that free labor is more economical. I admit that in some of the islands, especially the smaller ones, the landed proprietors have been great sufferers, and their estates have become depreciated in a remarkable manner, owing to a new direction of labor. But I am disposed to think that their misfortunes have, in great part, been brought on themselves, by their injudicious conduct. In the first instance, they paid the freed laborers at a low rate, and thus tempted them to emigrate to the larger Colonies, where higher remuneration was offered for labor; as in Trinidad and Demerara. Next, they endeavored to keep them at home, by allowing them to have as much land as they chose, and to keep as many cattle as they chose, without payment. This did, indeed, keep them at home; but its tendency was to keep them from laboring on the estates of the proprietors. They found it more for their interest to cultivate land on their own account.

"Sometimes, a single fact will prove more convincing than a multiplicity of arguments. I will state one fact, of which I am assured on the best authority. *The value of land in Barbadoes is so much increased since emancipation, that an estate will now sell for as much as it did formerly, when the slaves necessary for its cultivation were included in the purchase.* Who would have believed this to be possible, before slavery was abolished?

"Now let us compare the moral condition of the population with what it was previous to emancipation. It is admitted that, in the time of slavery, planters, attorneys, managers, merchants, etc., were licentious. Concubinage was common, and not held in discredit. There was a looseness of conduct and conversation, which could not fail to have an injurious effect on the mind. Youth was particularly exposed to this degrading and enervating influence, when there was no check to indulgence, no call to exercise control; when too often a gentleman's house was a kind of brothel, and when instances occurred of planters keeping in slavery their own offspring by slave mothers. From what I have seen and heard, the higher classes of the white population now appear to be exemplary in their conduct. A natural change has also taken place with regard to the emancipated race. Formerly, a colored woman esteemed it an honor to be the kept mistress of a white man. Now, she considers it disreputable; and few such connections are found. Marriage is more common among the black and colored people. The understanding is, that marriage is right, and concubinage wrong. There is still a good deal of irregular connection among them; the marriage tie is loose, and the senses little under the control of principle. But these remarks apply to the *older* portion of the population, whose habits were formed in slavery, when the marriage ceremony was not permitted, and when chastity was not known, even by name. I believe they do not apply to the rising generation, a certain proportion of whom have come under the influence of moral and religious training. The children of the laborers manifest great facility in learning at school; and the men have great aptitude in learning whatever they take an interest in, belonging to their trades and occupations; such as the use of implements in husbandry, and improved methods in the useful arts."

Dr. Davy states that three-fourths of the laborers in Antigua had cottages of their own, and small freeholds. Small as that island is, there were, at the time he wrote, about eighty-seven villages, all built by emancipated laborers, near the estates on which they were formerly chattels. He says: "It is a mistake, often committed, to suppose the African is by nature indolent, less inclined to work than the European. He who has witnessed, as I have, their indefatigable and provident industry, will be disposed perhaps to overrate, rather than underrate, the activity of the negroes."

In 1857, the Governor of Tobago published this statement: "I deny that the peasantry are abandoned to slothful habits. On the contrary, I assert that a more industrious class does not exist in the world; at least, when they are working for themselves."

When Louis Philippe sent Commissioners to the British West Indies, to inquire into the state of things, with a view to emancipation in the French Colonies, they published a Report, from which I translate the following extract: "In Guiana, some planters declare the impossibility of getting along with the existing system. Others, on the contrary, assure us that they never want for laborers; they praise the assiduity of the blacks, and say they produce as much as under the former system. So much for the *old* planters. But when we consult the *new* planters, men who know coerced labor only by tradition, we find among *them* entire unanimity. They all tell us that the labor is satisfactory, and that their agricultural operations succeed well."

Rev. Henry Bleby has been a missionary in the West Indies for thirty years. He resided there before emancipation and since. On the 1st of August, 1858, he delivered an address at Abington, Mass., from which I extract the following: "Since I have been here, I have heard that emancipation is understood to have been a failure. I am prepared to give that statement an unqualified contradiction. In no sense whatever has the emancipation of the slaves in the British Colonies proved a failure. I am at present laboring as a minister among the colored churches in Barbadoes, and I can tell you that never, even in the most palmy days of slavery, was there such prosperity as now. This year, a long drought has lessened the crop of sugar; yet they have raised more than double the amount of produce they ever raised under slavery; and with no greater amount of labor, than in the time of slavery. You cannot get an acre of land, in any part of the island, for less than four or five hundred dollars. In my own neighborhood an estate of not more than two or three hundred acres was sold for nearly $90,000 in your money; paid in cash. The case is the same in Antigua, where I lived three years. A member of my own church there bought an estate, which was sold under a decree of Chancery for $24,225. He has taken off three valuable crops, which have more than repaid the original purchase money; and he has been offered $48,450 for the property, and refused to take it. *That* is the kind of ruin that has come upon the West Indies because of emancipation!

"As for the moral condition of Barbadoes, I believe the criminal statistics, for the last five or six years, would compare, without disadvantage, with any country under heaven. We seldom hear of any thing like serious crimes. Intemperance is not prevalent among the people. I have a membership of seventeen hundred colored persons, and, during the last two years, I have not had one single case of intemperance reported to me. Every sabbath our churches are crowded with people anxious to receive instruction. I know of no people in the world who will make such efforts, and exercise such self-denial, to obtain education for their children, as the people of Barbadoes. One of my colored church members had just finished manufacturing his little portion of sugar, grown on part of the half-acre of land on which his house stood, and on which he raised provisions for his family; and he brought me six dollars in advance, as school fees for his four children the next twelve months. It is the only instance I ever knew of a man in *his* condition pre-paying the education of his children for a year. It is a falsehood that emancipation has failed to improve the condition of the colored race. Throughout the West Indies, in every island, the condition of the people is incomparably superior to what it was in slavery. Some say if it has not ruined the laborers, it has ruined the planters. I deny that statement, as plainly as I deny the other. Emancipation proved a blessing, instead of a curse, to the proprietors. What I have told you concerning the prices of land are facts that speak volumes in regard to the sort of ruin brought upon British planters by emancipation."

Lord Stanley, now Earl of Derby, in a despatch, dated February, 1842, says: " Experience has shown, what reason would anticipate, that the industry of the negro, like that of all mankind, is drawn out just in proportion to the interest he has in his labor." Lord John Russell declared in one of his public speeches: " None of the most inveterate opponents of our recent measures of emancipation allege that the negroes have turned robbers, or plunderers, or bloodthirsty insurgents. What appears from their statements is that they have become shopkeepers and petty traders, hucksters, and small freeholders. A blessed change this, which Providence has enabled us to accomplish !"

Sir Francis Hincks, formerly Prime Minister of Canada, is Governor of the Windward Islands, which comprise Barbadoes, St. Vincent, Grenada, St. Lucia, and Tobago. He is distinguished for financial ability, and practical good sense as a statesman. Being on a visit to England, he was present at an anniversary meeting in London, August 1st, 1859 ; on which occasion, he offered the following resolution : " That, on the twenty-fifth anniversary of the abolition of slavery in the British Colonies, this meeting joyfully records its satisfaction in the retrospect of that great act of national justice and sound policy ; and emphatically affirm that the emancipated population of those Colonies have triumphantly vindicated their right to freedom, and the justice of the Act of Emancipation, by the signal progress they have since made, morally, religiously, and politically."

In speaking to this Resolution, His Excellency said: "It is not denied by anybody in the West Indies that the good results of emancipation on the social condition of the people have been very great. In Barbadoes, the progress has been especially marked. I know of no people of the laboring class anywhere, who have done so much for the education of their children, as the people of Barbadoes; and results of the most gratifying character are to be seen in the social habits and mental acquirements of the people. I believe the planters themselves are convinced of the good results of emancipation. There can be no doubt in the minds of any, who investigate the subject, that slave labor is much dearer than free labor. I wish it to be understood that I have formed my opinion after full inquiry into the circumstances of every British Colony, regarding which I could obtain information.

"Let me deal at once with the popular delusion that the African Creole is naturally indolent; for that it *is* a delusion, I have no doubt whatever. My opinion is in accordance with all that I have heard from the clergymen of the various Protestant churches, as well as from those of the Church of Rome. It is likewise in accordance with the opinions expressed by the stipendiary magistrates generally, as I have found them in official documents. A Barbadoes proprietor, who stands high in the estimation of all who know him, writes to me thus: 'There never was a greater mistake, than to suppose the negro will not work for hire. No man is more sensitive to that stimulus, or works more readily, more cheerfully, or more effectually, for the hope of reward. It is perfectly astonishing how much a negro can do, when he is under the influence of a wholesome stimulus; and how little he will do, when that is removed.'" Gov. Hincks said: "I willingly admit that there has been a considerable withdrawal of labor from sugar cultivation in some of the Colonies, owing to a variety of causes. Among those causes, I am inclined to think that, next to the *tenure of land*, the *insolvency of the proprietors* has been the chief. I have never been able to trace an instance in which an estate has gone out of cultivation owing to want of *labor;* but I have heard of many cases in which estates have been abandoned for want of *capital;* and of some estates on which the laborers have been dismissed with wages several months in arrear. The only wonder is, that with such a land-tenure as that which exists in the West Indies, a single laborer has remained on the sugar estates. It is a tenure by the month, subject to ejectment by the owner. If the tenant has notice to quit, while his crops are growing, he is obliged to take for them whatever price the proprietor appraises them at. If the tenant himself gives notice of intention to leave, he is obliged to sacrifice his crops altogether. The obvious tendency of this is to drive laborers from sugar cultivation to places where they can get land of their own. If I were proprietor of a sugar estate, I would devote one-fourth, or one-third, of the cane land on the estate to the laborers. I would give them a good tenure; for instance, leases renewable forever, with a right to buy, at such a number of years' purchase as might be agreed upon. I would make it the interest of my laborers to occupy, or buy, land near my cane lands, instead of at a distance. I would trust to their admitted sagacity to cultivate the product that would *pay* them best. I would have a labor market at my door; and I would have the spare time of my laborers employed in growing a a product, which must be brought to my works to be manufactured. Even if the result should be that all my land was rented or sold, I should still make ample profit by my manufactory. Such, however, in my opinion, would not be the case. The large proprietor would still be the principal cultivator of the land, and the small one would combine labor on the estates with labor on his own land in growing the cane; as is the case in Barbadoes. But this common-sense view of the subject has not been generally taken. In Barbadoes alone so far as my knowledge extends, the laborers on the large estates cultivate the sugar cane on their own grounds; and this is one of the reasons why the laborers in Barbadoes cannot be attracted elsewhere. There, the laborer is dependent on the proprietor for the manufacture of his little crop of canes, while the proprietor is dependent on him for labor, when it is required. This mutual dependence has produced the best results."

When Gov. Hincks visited Canada, April, 1859, he received an address from the Association for the Education of the Colored People. I make the following extract from his reply: "While it is my own deliberate opinion that a very large amount of labor now wasted in the West Indies, or less profitably employed, could be obtained for the cultivation of sugar, I am not prepared to admit that the success of the great measure of emancipation is to be tested in this way. The true test, it seems to me, is the progress of the African race. The best proof of the industry of that race is that large numbers have acquired, and are acquiring, large properties. They are amenable to the laws, anxious for the education of their children, and good and loyal subjects to the queen. There is still vast room for improvement; but I certainly concur in the following statement by the Lord Bishop of Barbadoes, a prelate esteemed and respected by all who have the advantage of his friendship: 'I certainly think we have great reason to say, especially in Barbadoes, that the advantages resulting from the abolition of slavery have been quite as great as we could reasonably expect, in so short a time; much greater, indeed, than the most sanguine among us, I believe, ever anticipated.'"

Mr. Charles Tappan, of Boston, visited the West Indies, in the autumn of 1857; and in January, 1858, Gov. Hincks wrote him a letter, dated Barbadoes, in answer to some questions that had been addressed to him. It was published in the *National Era*, and some other papers. I make the following extracts from it. "With regard to the complaint against the negroes, that they are indolent, and have abandoned the sugar plantations, I admit that, in several of the British Colonies, the planters would generally vehemently maintain the correctness of the charge. I am, however, bound to affirm that, after a most patient investigation, I have been unable to arrive at such a conclusion. There is no doubt that the condition of the laboring class in Barbadoes ought to be worse than in any of the other Colonies; for land is exorbitantly dear, being from $400 to $600 an acre; while wages are from tenpence to a shilling (twenty-four cents) a day. There are only five working days in the week, except during crop time. With all these disadvantages, the small proprietors in Barbadoes, those holding less than five acres of land, have increased in sixteen years, from about 1,100 to 3,537. I doubt very much whether such a proof of industrious habits could be furnished with regard to a similar class of laborers in any other country in the world. I adduce this remarkable fact to prove that there has been no want of industry in this island, on the part of the Creoles of African descent.

"In all those Colonies where the sugar estates have been partially abandoned, we must look to other causes than the indolence of the laborers. In all those Colonies, land is abundant and comparatively cheap; and I need not remind any one acquainted with the settlement of land in America, that where land is abundant and cheap, labor will be scarce and dear. The negroes in Guiana and Trinidad pursue the same course as poor Irish emigrants in Canada, or the United States; they endeavor to get land of their own, and to become proprietors instead of laborers. Unfortunately, the planters have never adopted a policy calculated to retain laborers on their plantations. At least, such is my opinion. I am fully convinced that the abandonment of the estates is more owing to the tenure, on which alone planters would lease land, than to any other cause.

"In this island, there can be no doubt whatever, that emancipation has been a great boon to all classes. The estates are much better cultivated, and more economically. Real estate has increased in price, and is a more certain and advantageous investment, than in the time of slavery. The proprietor of an estate, containing three hundred acres of land, twelve miles from the shipping port, informs me that the estate, during slavery, required two hundred and thirty slaves, and produced on an average, one hundred and forty hogheads of sugar. It is now worked by ninety free laborers, and the average product the last seven years has been one hundred and ninety hogheads. During slavery, this estate was worth £15,000 ($72,675); under the apprenticeship, it was sold for £25,000 ($121,125); the present proprietor purchased it a few years ago, for £30,000 ($145,350), which I have no doubt he could obtain for it at any moment. I could multiply instances, where the results have been similar.

"The improvement which has taken place in the religious condition of all classes, and the progress of education, are quite equal to what could have been reasonably expected. You have yourself made the acquaintance of men, who were once slaves, who are now in independent circumstances, and enjoying a large share of public respect. It is impossible to compare the present statistics of crime with those during slavery; for then the great bulk of ordinary offences, such as petty thefts and assaults, were not brought before magistrates, but summarily punished by managers and overseers on the estates. That there is much greater security for person and property now, than during slavery, does not admit of a doubt."

Never was an experiment more severely tested, than that of emancipation in the West Indies. It seems as if God intended to prove to the world that the vitality of freedom was indestructible. In addition to the general state of insolvency to which slavery had reduced the planters, and the difficulties attending the commencement of all great changes in the social system, there were an unusual number of fortuitous calamities. In 1843, an earthquake made dreadful devastation in the Leeward Islands. Out of one hundred and seventy-two sugar mills in Antigua, one hundred and seventeen were demolished, or nearly so. A third of the houses in St. John's were flung down, and the remainder too much injured to be habitable. Then came a hurricane which blew down churches, uprooted trees, destroyed a great many houses and huts, did immense damage to the sugar canes. And the crowning misfortune of all, was a series of severe droughts, year after year. Between 1840 and 1849, there were only two seasons when the crops did not suffer terribly for rain. Under such a combination of disasters the anxieties and sufferings of West India proprietors must have been very severe indeed; and there, as elsewhere, there were plenty of people ready and eager to attribute all their troubles to emancipation. Yet such is the recuperative power of freedom, that Commissioners who went to Guiana in 1850, to inquire into the condition of things, reported: "Every symptom of change for the better is apparent. Cultivation has extended and crops increased. The laboring population are working more steadily, and evince signs of speedy improvement."

In the first part of this Tract it has been mentioned that in twelve years, during slavery, the laboring class in eleven of the islands had *decreased* more than 60,000. In the
5

twelve years following emancipation, in ten Colonies there was an *increase* of more than 54,000. That fact alone is a significant indication of the vast change for the better in their condition.

The following statistics I copy from an able article in the *Edinburgh Review*, April, 1859. They are quoted from the Colonial Reports:—

Barbadoes. In ten years, "between 1842 and 1852, increase of sugar exported, is 27,240 hogheads." The Report for 1851, states, "There has been more sugar shipped from this island this year, than in any one year since it has been peopled; and it is a remarkable fact that there will be more *laborers'* sugar made this year, than previously. By laborers' sugar is meant that raised by the negroes on their own patches of ground, and sent to the proprietor's mill for manufacture." The Report for 1853 announces "vast increase in trade. So far the success of cultivation by free labor is unquestionable." Report for 1858: "A great increase in the value of the exports." "The large proportion of land acquired by the laboring classes furnishes striking evidence of their industry."

Bahamas. In 1851, the Governor reports, "a great and important change for the better," in the condition of the people; which he mainly attributes to "improved education." The rapidity with which these islands are advancing is indicated by the fact that the exports and imports increased in one year, from 1854 to 1855, £102,924 ($498,666.78).

Grenada. Returns in 1851 and 1852, show an increase of trade, amounting to £88,414 ($428,355.83). Report of 1858: "Contentment appears to pervade all classes of the community." "A proprietary body, of considerable magnitude and importance, has already risen from the laboring class." "State of the finances most satisfactory." "A greatly extended surface is covered by sugar cultivation." A considerable increase is noted in the exports of sugar, rum, and cocoa. Some remarks on the want of labor.

Antigua. — Reports for 1858: "Satisfactory evidence is afforded, by the Revenue Returns, of increase of trade and mercantile business, consequent upon the revival of agricultural prosperity." (There had been a depression in consequence of a great fall in the price of sugar in 1847.)

Dominica. — Report for 1853: "The steady maintenance of production is full of promise as to the future." Report for 1857: "The exports show a considerable increase." "Very considerable increase in revenue, and an equally marked improvement in the amount of imports." In the Report for 1858, the Governor speaks of the growing independence of the laborers, manifested "in the small patches of canes, and little wooden mills here and there dotting the plains around."

Guiana. — In 1852. the Governor reports that the fall in the price of sugar, in 1847 and 1848 (owing to the repeal of the tariff), was "so sudden and enormous, as to have almost annihilated the Colony, at that crisis." But he goes on to state that "the revenue is now flourishing, population augmenting, education spreading, crime diminishing, and trade increasing."

Montserrat. — In 1853, the Governor reports "increase of confidence, enterprise, and industry." "The improved and improving state of the community is allowed on all hands." "No island in these seas exhibits a more decisive tendency to social and moral regeneration and improvement. The rural population are quiet, contented, and orderly."

Nevis. — (This is a very small island; about the size of a common New England town.) Report for 1857 : "The roads appear as if the greater part of the population had new clothed themselves; and in the harbor, so often deserted, I now count ten ships of considerable burden." "There appears now to be at work an industrious spirit of improvement."

St. Kitts. — Report for 1856: A larger quantity of sugar is produced now than in the time of slavery" (though on a smaller area). Report for 1858 : "The agricultural prospects of the island are most encouraging. Its financial condition continues satisfactory; so do the education returns. Attendance in schools is steadily increasing. Crime is steadily diminishing. In one year, from 1856 to 1857, trade increased £106,233" ($514,642.88).

St. Lucia. — Report for 1853 : "At no period of her history, has there been a greater breadth of land under cultivation, than at the present moment." Between the four years ending 1842, and the four years ending 1856, the increase of sugar exported was 1,803,618 pounds.

St. Vincent. — In 1857, the Governor describes "a really sound and healthy state of the Colony at present, and a cheering and promising prospect for the future." He describes the rising villages, the growing number of freeholders and leaseholders, and the steady progressive increase in the value of imports. In one year, from 1856 to 1857, imports and exports increased £156,633 ($758,886.88); and he expressly attributes it to "increased cultivation and prosperity." In 1858, he describes the Colony as "in a most satisfactory state." "Agricultural operations largely extended." "Anticipations of continued progress and prosperity fully realized."

Tobago. — The accounts had been dismal in 1852 and 1853; but an improved financial system was adopted in 1856, the result of which was a Report in 1858 announcing a "marked improve-

ment in the revenue returns." The Governor describes the laborers as " well-behaved and industrious."
Tortola. — This island, under slavery, exported 15,559 cwt. of sugar. Now it exports none at all. But the change is wholly an advantage. It is remarkably well adapted for the raising of stock. " The people, with few exceptions, are owners of cattle, which they dispose of to great advantage." " The laborers appear fully sensible of the advantages of education to their children, and the latter manifest a great desire to benefit by the opportunities offered them."
Trinidad is highly flourishing. In 1852, the crop was the largest ever shipped from the island; and it has been extending since. The whole trade greatly increased since slavery. The Report for 1853 speaks of " marked improvement in the cultivation of the sugar estates." Export of sugar rose from an average of 310,797 cwt. under slavery, to 426,042 cwt. in the seven years ending 1854.

The writer in the *Edinburgh Review* says : " These specific accounts of the several islands are borne out by the statistics and Reports that relate to our West Indies *en masse.* Lest it should be thought that these extracts are carefully culled, to produce a particular impression, and that if the reader had the *whole* Reports before him, he would find complaints and lamentations, we may at once say that they appear to us to be fair samples of the views entertained by the Governors, and also by other gentlemen acquainted with the West Indies. The language of complaint is no longer heard. Throughout these Colonies, hope and congratulation seem to have taken the place of irritation and despair. In all cases, the later the Report, the more gratifying it is found to be.

" To men of business, one fact will seem almost enough by itself to show the sound commercial state of these Colonies; viz., that, in the year 1857, the Colonial Bank received bills from the West Indies to the amount of more than £1,300,-000 ($6,298,500); and less than £8,000 ($38,760) were returned. Nor was there a single failure in the West India trade, during the severe commercial crisis of that year. Furthermore, coffee, cotton, wool, sugar, rum, and cocoa, are all exported in increasing quantities. The total exports from Great Britain to the West Indies in 1857 were valued at half a milliom more ($2,422,500) than the average of the preceding ten years."

Mr. C. Buxton made a speech in the British House of Commons, March, 1859, in which he said : "Because labor is free, and trade is free, the West Indies are now rising to a pitch of wealth and happiness unknown before. It would be impossible for me to lay before the House the immense mass of evidence, which demonstrates that fact. I am assured of it by mercantile men, I find it strongly set forth in the Reports from the Governors of the Islands, and in the statistics furnished by the Board of Trade. In the four years between 1853 and 1857, there has been an increase in the exports and imports of the West Indies and Guiana of £4,500,000 ($21,802,500). Considering what mere specks these islands look on the map of America, it is astonishing that their trade to and fro, in the year 1857, should actually amount to £10,735,000 ($52,011,075). It is altogether absurd to suppose this prosperity is owing to the immigration of a few thousand laborers; and in fact the islands which have received no immigrants are quite as flourishing as those that have. Interested parties describe the negroes as barbarous and idle; but I find ample evidence that they are living in a high degree of industry and comfort; though I admit that they somewhat prefer working on freeholds they have purchased, to laboring for hire."

The *Edinburgh Review* concludes its array of evidence, by saying : " A long and thorough investigation of the case has borne us irresistibly to the conclusion that, merely as a dry question of *economy*, emancipation has *paid ;* that it was an act of prudence, for which we, as a nation of shopkeepers, need not blush before that golden god, whom we are thought to worship. so eagerly. Slavery and monopoly were bearing the West Indies to ruin. Under free labor and free trade they are rising to wealth. They are yearly enriching us more and more with the wealth of their fertile soil. Instead of being the plague of statesmen and the disgrace of England, they are becoming invaluable possessions of the British crown. Never did any deed of any nation show more signally that to do right is the truest *prudence,* than the great deed of Emancipation."

CHAPTER V.

JAMAICA.*

I HAVE placed Jamaica in a section by itself, because emancipation has there worked less prosperously than elsewhere, and the reasons for it need some explanation. I have already mentioned causes which were bringing all the West Indies to ruin, previous to emancipation. These operated as powerfully in Jamaica as elsewhere. They were cursed with the same coercive system, which seems ingeniously contrived to make laborers lazy and shiftless, and to array them in the most stubborn opposition to their employers. There was among the white population the same haughty contempt for useful occupations, which inevitably brings extravagance and dissipation in its train. There was the same expensive retinue of attorneys, managers, and bookkeepers, with their mistresses, servants, and horses, to be supported out of the estate. There was the same neglect and fraud, arising from the absence of proprietors; for "nine-tenths of the land in Jamaica was owned by absentees, mostly residing in England." There was the same injudicious system of apportioning the soil into large plantations, to the utter exclusion of small farmers; for slavery always renders the existence of a middling class impossible. There was the same desperate game of borrowing and mortgaging, ending in universal insolvency. Mr. Bigelow, one of the editors of the *New York Evening Post*, visited Jamaica in 1850, and carefully examined into the state of things. He says: "The island was utterly insolvent the day the Emancipation Bill passed. Nearly every estate was mortgaged for more than it was worth, and was liable for more interest than it could possibly pay. It will not be dis-

---

* The population of Jamaica, at the time of emancipation, was 37,000 whites; 311,692 slaves; 55,000 free colored people.

puted by any, who are at all informed on the subject, that the whole real estate under culture in Jamaica, in 1832, would not have sold for enough to pay off encumbrances. This fact must have been disclosed sooner or later, even if slavery had been permitted to continue. Bankruptcy was inevitable; and the rapid depreciation of real estate would, of course, have been one of the first fruits of such a catastrophe. The Emancipation Act did not cause, it only precipitated, a result, which was inevitable. It compelled a balance to be struck between the debtors and the creditors, which revealed, rather than begat, the poverty which now no effort can conceal."

The Export Tables show a decrease of sugar, in ten years, ending 1830, of 201,843 hogsheads.

These drawbacks Jamaica had in common with the other Colonies; except, perhaps, that the load of debt was somewhat heavier there than elsewhere. Why then have her complaints been so much louder and more prolonged, than those of her neighbors? I think the strongest reason is to be found in the fact that the spirit of slavery was more violent and unyielding there than in the other Colonies. There was more bitter hostility between masters and slaves; manifesting itself in shocking barbarities on one side, and frequent riots and insurrections on the other. There was a more furious opposition to abolition, and a more stubborn determination to make it operate badly, if possible. The great body of the planters had predicted ruin, and they seemed resolved that they *would* be ruined, rather than prove false prophets. Dr. Coke, one of the missionaries, says: "The persecutions we have experienced in Jamaica far exceed, *very* far, all the persecutions we have experienced in all the other islands unitedly considered." Those who opened their houses to these religious teachers, in many instances, narrowly escaped being stoned to death. Rev. Mr. Bleby says: "Being determined to perpetuate slavery, they resolved to do all they could to get rid of Christianity, and keep their people in heathen darkness. The whole white population of Jamaica banded themselves together in an Association, which they called The Colonial Union; the avowed object of which was to drive every instructor of the negroes from the island. Eighteen of our churches were levelled with the ground. They dragged the missionaries to prison, got false witnesses to swear against them, treated them with brutal violence, and did every thing they could to put an end to their labors." One of the Methodist missionaries died in a dungeon, in consequence of the brutal treatment he had received from violent proslavery men.

Another cause for the slow progress of improvement in Jamaica is assigned by the writer in the *Edinburgh Review;* viz., "the superlative badness of its government." Taxation has been, and is oppressive, and the financial arrangements are said to be very injudicious. As late as 1854, the Governor, Sir Charles Grey, declared, "There is no system or consistency whatever in the conduct of the financial affairs of the Colony; nor any recognized organ of government, or legislature, which has the power to bring about effective and comprehensive changes."

There was a small minority of planters and merchants, who regretted the violence and blind policy of the majority; but they would have risked their property, if not their lives, by venturing to express disapprobation. The excitement was prodigiously increased in 1832, by a formidable attempt at insurrection, in consequence of the numerous meetings and inflamed speeches of the planters, from which the slaves got the idea that the British government had made them free, and that their masters were acting in opposition to it.

Such was the community into which the modified freedom called apprenticeship was ushered on the 1st of August, 1834. In an address delivered in Massachusetts, 1858, the Rev. Mr. Bleby said: "I was in Jamaica when slavery was abolished. This day, twenty-four years ago, I stood up late at night in one of the churches under my charge. It was a very large church; and the aisles, the gallery stairs, the communion place, the pulpit stairs, were all crowded; and there were thousands of people round the building, at every open door and window, looking in. It was ten o'clock at night, on the 31st of July. We thought it right and proper that our Christian people should receive their freedom, as a boon from God, in the house of prayer; and we gathered them together in the church for a midnight service. Our mouths had been closed about slavery up to that time.

We could not quote a passage that had reference even to *spiritual* emancipation, without endangering our lives. The planters had a law of 'constructive treason,' that doomed any man to death, who made use of language tending to excite a desire for liberty among the slaves; and they found treason in the Bible, and sedition in the hymns of Watts and Wesley; and we had to be very careful how we used them. You may imagine with what feelings I saw myself emancipated from this thraldom, and free to proclaim 'liberty to the captive, and the opening of prison doors to them that were bound.' I took for my text, 'Proclaim liberty throughout all the land, unto all the inhabitants thereof! It shall be a jubilee unto you.' A few minutes before midnight, I requested all the people to kneel down in silent prayer to God, as befitting the solemnity of the hour. I looked down upon them as they knelt. The silence was broken only by sobs of emotion, which it was impossible to repress. The clock began to strike. It was the knell of slavery, in all the British possessions! It proclaimed liberty to 800,000 human beings! When I told them they might rise, what an outburst of joy there was among that mass of people! The clock had ceased to strike, and they were slaves no longer! Mothers were hugging their babes to their bosoms, old white-headed men embracing their children, and husbands clasping their wives in their arms. By and by, all was still again, and I gave out a hymn. You may imagine the feelings with which these people, just emerging into freedom, shouted — for they literally *shouted*,

"'Send the glad tidings o'er the sea!
His chains are broke, the slave is free!'"

THE PLANTERS' STATE OF MIND, IN 1837.

Three years after this event, Mr. Thome visited Jamaica. He constantly encountered men full of the old slave-holding prejudices. They gave doleful pictures of the ingratitude and laziness of the negroes. Things were bad enough, they said, but they were sure they would be much worse when the laborers were entirely free, in 1840. It was in vain to try to comfort them by telling them how well immediate emancipation had worked in Antigua. They listened incredulously, and returned to their old statement, that negroes would not work, unless they were flogged. When they were freed, they would, of course, rob, murder, starve, do any thing, rather than labor. "There would be scenes of carnage and ruin, unparalleled in modern times." Mr. Thomson, one of the local magistrates of St. Andrews, belonged to this old school, who up to the last moment had resisted any change of system. Yet he wound up his direful predictions by denouncing slavery. He said man was naturally a tyrant, and it could not be denied that under slavery the most horrible cruelties had been practised. He admitted that he had formerly been very averse to sleeping on any of his estates in the country. If circumstances compelled him to spend a night there in the midst of his slaves, he not only bolted the door, but took the precaution to barricade it. Now, he had no fears. One thing he was ready to say in favor of negroes; they were a very temperate people; it was a rare thing to see one of them drunk. Similar admissions were made by other planters of the old school; but they all persisted in the opinion that there would be trouble, in 1840, when the masters lost what restraining power they now had. The very best thing to be expected was that the negroes "would all retire to the woods, plant merely yams enough to keep them alive, and before long all retrograde into African barbarism."

It is obvious that men so completely under the dominion of passion and prejudice were not likely to use power judiciously; and, unfortunately, the apprenticeship system, which was intended as a salutary preparation for freedom, proved nothing but a source of exasperation to both parties. It took from the slaves certain privileges, which the laws and customs had previously secured to them, and it did not compensate for this by giving them the stimulus and the advantages of wages. On the other hand, the new system fettered the masters, to a degree that kept them in a state of irritation, while it left them power enough to manifest their ill-temper by perpetual annoyances to their servants. In the preceding pages I have given the opinion of various planters and magistrates, that this system worked badly in all the Colonies; but it was pre-eminently mischievous in

Jamaica, because there the disease of slavery was of a peculiarly malignant type. The laborers were no longer *property;* and, with hard masters, no *other* claim to consideration remained when that was gone. They had made up their minds that the negroes would all quit work in 1840, and all they cared for was to get all they could out of their bones and sinews *before* that time. All children under six years old were unconditionally free. What consequence was it to the planters, whether "the little black devils" (as they called them) lived or died? Among the apprenticed laborers was a mother, who was let out by her master. Her child became alarmingly ill; and her employer said it was not his business to provide doctor or nurse. With the little sufferer in her arms, she went to her master for aid; but he turned her into the streets. It was the business of the people to take care of their own "brats," now. She obtained shelter in the house of a colored man, and there the child died before morning.

A continual system of provocation was kept up. Masters and their white subordinates would take produce from the provision-grounds of the apprentices without paying them. In fits of anger, they would sometimes destroy their little gardens, or take them away when the crops were growing. The magistrates were overwhelmed with complaints, most of them of a petty character. An overseer would call out, "Work faster, you black rascal! or I'll strike you." If the apprentice answered, "You *can't* strike me now," he was dragged before a magistrate, and punished for insolence. The fact that the power of punishment was transferred by law from master to magistrates proved very insufficient protection; for the magistrates were generally planters, or the friends of planters. If one of them manifested a disposition to be humane, or even just, toward the apprentices, machinations were immediately on foot to get him turned out of office. The result was, that a large proportion of them were unprincipled men, the mere selfish tools of despotism. The negroes expressed it concisely by saying : "If massa say flog 'em, he flog 'em ; if massa say send 'em to de tread-mill, he send 'em." Their common complaint of magistrates was, "Dey be poisoned wid massa's turtle-soup;" that being their way of defining the influence of good dinners. One of the missionaries complained to Mr. Thome, of a whipping machine ingeniously contrived for torture, and placed very near his house. He said when news came that the Governor was about to visit the village, the magistrate caused the machine to be removed and hidden among the bushes. Mr. Thome was present at a weekly court, where a just and humane magistrate presided. He says : " Managers, overseers, and bookkeepers, all set upon him like bloodhounds on a stag. They seemed to gnash their teeth upon him in their impotent rage. He assured us that he met with similar indignities on most of the estates, every time he held his courts. From what we saw that day, we were convinced that only very fearless and conscientious men could be faithful magistrates in Jamaica." Mr. Thome tells an anecdote related to him by the special magistrate in whose presence it occurred. It shows how hard it was, for men long accustomed to arbitrary power, to submit to the salutary restraints of law. The magistrate had fined a manager $108 for various acts of oppression complained of and proved by his apprentices. The culprit requested permission to speak ; which being granted, he broke forth, in an agony of passion, "O my God! Has it come to this? Is my conduct to be questioned by these people? Is my authority to be interfered with by strangers? O my God! my God!" He fell back into the arms of one of his bookkeepers, and was carried out of court in a convulsion fit.

The Rev. James Phillipo, who was a Baptist Missionary in Jamaica for twenty years, says: " During the short period of two years, 60,000 apprentices received in the aggregate one quarter of a million of lashes ; and fifty thousand other punishments by the tread-wheel, the chain-gang, and other modes of legalized torture. Instead of diminution of the miseries of the negro population, there was a frightful addition to them ; inducing a degree of discontent and exasperation never manifested even under the previous system. Had it not been for the influence of the Governor, the missionaries, and some of the special magistrates, it would probably have broken out into open and general rebellion."

THE NEGROES' STATE OF MIND, IN 1837.

While Mr. Thome was travelling in the rural districts, he talked with many of the apprentices. He says: "They all thought the apprenticeship very hard; but still, on the whole it was rather better than slavery. Then they were 'killed *too* bad.' It was all slash, slash! Now, they couldn't be flogged unless the magistrate said so. Still, some masters were very hard; and many of the apprentices were so badly used, that they ran away into the woods. They should all be glad when freedom came.

"They gave a heart-sickening account of the cruelties of the tread-mill. Sometimes their wives were tied on the wheel when they were in a state of pregnancy. They suffered a great deal from that; but they couldn't help it. We asked why they didn't complain to the magistrates. They replied, that the magistrates wouldn't take any notice of their complaints; and besides, it only made the masters treat them worse. One of them said, ' We go to de magistrate, and den, when we come back, massa do all him can to vex us. He wingle (tease) us, and wingle us, and wingle us; de bookkeeper curse us and treaten us; de constable he scold us and call us hard names; and dey all try to make we mad; so we sometimes say someting wrong, and den dey take we to de magistrate for insolence.'

"We asked them what they thought of the household slaves being free in 1838, while *they* had to remain apprentices two years longer. They said, ' It bad enough; but we know de *law* make it so; and for peace' sake, we will be satisfy. But we murmur in we minds.' One of the magistrates told us that on several estates the house servants announced their determination to remain apprentices until the field hands were all free; giving as a reason, that they wanted all to have a jubilee together.

"We inquired whether they expected to do as they pleased when they were free. They answered, ' We couldn't live widout de *law*. In other countries, where dey is free, don't *dey* have de law?' We asked what they expected to do with the old and infirm. They said, ' We will support dem. Dey brought us up when we was pickaniny, and now we come trong, we must take care of dem.' We asked whether they would work when they were free. They replied, 'In slavery time, we work, *even* wid de whip; *now* we work till better; what tink we will do when we *free?* *Wont* we work when we get *paid!*' It was said so earnestly, we couldn't help acknowledging ourselves convinced. Some of them had to travel too far to market, to get back till Sunday. One of them said to us with tears in his eyes, 'I declare to you, massa, if de Lord only spare we to be free, we be much more 'ligious. We be wise to many more tings.' "

FAVORABLE TESTIMONY OF PLANTERS, IN 1837.

"At Amity Hall, Mr. Kirkland, the manager of the estate, introduced us to his wife and several lovely children. It was the first and the last *family circle* we saw in that licentious Colony. The motley groups of colored children which we found on other estates, revealed the domestic manners of the planters. Mr. Kirkland considered the abolition of slavery a great blessing to the Colony. He said the apprenticeship was a wretchedly bad system; but things moved smoothly on his estate. He said the negroes of Amity Hall had formerly borne the character of being the worst gang in the parish; and when he came to the estate, he found that half the truth had not been told of them. But they had become remarkably peaceful and subordinate. He said he looked forward to 1840, with the most sanguine hope. He believed complete freedom would be the regeneration of the island. Forty freemen would accomplish as much as eighty slaves. If any of the estates were abandoned by the laborers, it would be on account of the harsh treatment they received. He knew many cruel overseers, and he shouldn't be surprised if *they* lost a part of their laborers, or all of them.

"Mr. Gordon, the manager of Williamsfield estate, is among the fairest specimens of planters. He has a naturally generous disposition, which, like that of Mr. Kirkland, has outlived the witherings of slavery. He informed us that his people worked as well as they had done under slavery; and he had every reason to believe they would do still better after they were completely free. He said he often hired his people on Saturdays, and it was wonderful, with what increased vigor they worked when they were to receive wages. Fifty free men would do as much as a hundred slaves. He condemned the driving system, which was resorted to by a great many planters.

"Andrew Wright, Esq., proprietor of Green Wall estate, was described to us as a very amiable, kind man, who was never known to quarrel with any person in his life. He had a hundred and sixty apprentices at work, and said they were as peaceable and industrious as he could wish. He said where there was trouble with the people, he believed it was owing to bad management. He was quite confident that his laborers would not leave him after 1840.

"Mr. Briant, manager of Belvidere estate, said he had had no trouble with his apprentices. They did as much work, for the length of time, as they did during slavery; but the law allowed them a day and a half for themselves, and did not require them to work so early in the morning, or so late at night. He said the apprentices were not willing to work for their masters on Saturday, for the customary wages, which were about a quarter of a dollar. Upon inquiry, we ascertained that the reason was, they could make twice or three times as much by cultivating their provision-grounds and carrying the produce to market. At night, when they couldn't work on their grounds, he said they worked very cheerfully for their masters. Where there was mild management, he had no doubt the negroes would remain and work well.

"In Bath, we met with the proprietor of a coffee estate, who gave a very favorable account of his laborers. He said they were as orderly and industrious as he could desire; he had their confidence, and had no doubt he should retain it after they were entirely free. He felt assured that if the planters would only conduct in a proper manner, emancipation would prove a blessing to the whole Colony."

TESTIMONY OF MAGISTRATES IN 1837.

William H. Anderson, Esq., Solicitor General, made a written statement, from which I extract the following: "A very material change for the better has taken place in the sentiments of the community, since slavery was abolished.

Religion and education were formerly opposed, as subversive of the security of *property;* now, they are encouraged, in the most direct manner, as its best support. Many proprietors give land for schools and chapels; also subscriptions to a large amount. Had the negroes been entirely emancipated in 1834, they would have been much further advanced in 1840, than they can be at the end of the apprenticeship, through which both masters and servants are laboring heavily. That the negroes will work, if moderately compensated, no candid man can doubt. Their endurance for the sake of a very little gain is quite amazing; and they are very desirous to procure for themselves and families as large a share as possible of the comforts and decencies of life. I have not heard one man assert that it would be an advantage to return to slavery, even if it were practicable; and I believe the public begin to be convinced that slave labor is not the cheapest. In my opinion, the negroes are very acute in their perceptions of justice and injustice. They fully appreciate the benefits of equitable legislation, and would unreservedly submit to it, where they felt confidence in the purity of its administration. They are ardently attached to the British government, and would be so to the Colonial, were it to indicate any purposes of kindness or protection toward them; but hitherto the enactments with reference to them have been almost wholly coercive. They are very desirous for education and religious instruction; no man who has attended to the matter can gainsay that. Marriage was formerly unknown among them. Their masters considered them as so many brutes for labor and increase, and I fear they came to regard themselves so. But now concubinage is becoming quite disreputable, and many are marrying those with whom they formerly lived in that relation. The partial modification of slavery has been attended with so much improvement in all that constitutes the welfare and respectability of society, that I cannot doubt there would be an increase of the benefits, if there were a total abolition of all the old restrictions."

"Cheney Hamilton, Esq., one of the Special Magistrates for Port Royal, said there were three thousand apprentices in his district. They were as quiet and industrious as they ever were, and were always willing to work in their own time for wages. The district was never under better cultivation. The masters were doing nothing for the education of the apprentices. Their only object seemed to be to get as much work out of them as possible. The complaints brought before him mostly originated with the planters and were of a trivial nature, such as petty thefts and absence from work. He said if we would compare the complaints brought by overseers and apprentices against each other, we should see for ourselves which party was the most peaceable and law-abiding. Real estate is more valuable than before emancipation. Property is more secure, and capitalists, consequently, more ready to invest their funds."

From the written testimony of E. B. Lyon, Esq., Special Justice, I extract the following: "The estates of the Blue Mountain Valley, over which I preside, contain 4.227 apprentices. When I assumed the duties of a special magistrate, they were the most disorderly on the island. They were almost desperate from disappointment in finding their trammels under the new law nearly as burdensome as under the old, and their condition in many respects much more intolerable. But they submitted, in many instances, with the most extraordinary patience, to evils which were the more onerous, because inflicted under the affected sanction of a law, whose advent they expected would have been attended with a train of blessings. I succeeded in making satisfactory arrangements between the masters and apprentices; and no peasantry, in the most favored country on the globe, can have been more irreproachable in morals and conduct, than the majority of apprentices in that district, since the beginning of 1835. It has been my pleasant duty to report to the Governor, month after month, improvement in their manners and condition, and a greater amount of work than during slavery. That proprietors have confidence in the future is evinced by the expensive repair of buildings on various estates, the enlargement of works, and the high prices given for land, which would scarcely have commanded a purchaser at any price, during slavery. In my district, the apprentices are invariably willing to work on the estates for hire, during their own time. In no community in the world, is crime less prevalent. The offences brought before me are mostly of a trivial description; such as turning out late, or answering impatiently. In fact, the majority of apprentices on estates have quietly performed their duty and respected the laws. The apprenticeship has, I fear, retarded the rapidity with which civilization should have advanced, and sown the seeds of a feeling even more bitter than that which slavery had engendered."

TESTIMONY OF MISSIONARIES, IN 1837.

Rev. Mr. Crookes, of the Wesleyan Mission, said to Mr. Thome: "In many respects there has been a great improvement since the abolition of slavery. The obstacles to religious effort have been considerably diminished; but we owe that mainly to the protection of British law. I believe many of the planters would still persecute the missionaries, and tear down their chapels, if they dared. I abominate the apprentice system. At best, it is only mitigated slavery. I am convinced that immediate and entire emancipation would have been far better policy." The Rev. Jonathan Edmonson, and Rev. Mr. Wooldridge agreed in testifying that the planters generally, were doing "comparatively nothing to prepare the negroes for freedom." "Their sole object seemed to be to get as much work as possible out of them before 1840." "Their conduct was calculated to make the apprentices their bitter enemies."

The Wesleyan Missionary at Bath said: "There are some bad characters among the negroes, as there are everywhere, among all classes of people. But generally they are docile and well behaved. They are eager for instruction. After working all day, they come several miles to our evening schools, and stay cheerfully till nine o'clock. Mothers with sucking babes in their arms stand, night after night, in our classes, learning the alphabet. If they can obtain even the leaf of a book they make it their constant companion. They are very easily won by acts of kindness. Sometimes they burst into tears and say to the missionaries, 'Massa *so* kind! Me heart full.'"

Mr. Thome says: "While we were at Garden River Valley, we attended service in the Baptist Chapel, on the summit of a high mountain, overlooking the sea. Seen from the valley below, it appears to topple on the brink of a frightful precipice. As we ascended the steep and winding road, we saw throngs of apprentices, coming from many miles round, in every direction. The men halted in the thick woods to put on their shoes, which they brought in their hands up the mountain, and the women to draw on their white stockings. Mr. Kingdon, the pastor asked us to address his people, and we cannot soon forget the scene that followed. We had scarcely uttered a sentence, expressive of our sympathy with their condition, and our interest in their temporal and spiritual welfare, before the whole audience began to weep. Some sobbed, others cried aloud; insomuch that for a time we were unable to proceed. When we spoke of it afterwards to their pastor, he said, 'The idea that a stranger and a foreigner should take an interest in their welfare stirred the deep fountains of their hearts. They are so unaccustomed to hear such language from white people, that it fell upon them like rain on the parched earth.'"

JAMAICA BETWEEN 1837 AND 1846.

As time passed on, the conviction deepened in the minds of magistrates, missionaries, and the more reflecting among the planters, that slavery, by its very nature, did not admit of any modification. The apprenticeship system proved "hateful to the slave, obnoxious to the master, and perplexing to the magistrates." Some of the apprentices bought their time; and their orderly, industrious habits afterward confirmed the growing impression that entire emancipation was the *best policy*. The Marquis of Sligo, the humane and just Governor of Jamaica, was a large proprietor, and he manifested his sentiments by liberating all his apprentices. His example had great influence. Public opinion was again roused in England. Petitions from all classes poured into Parliament, begging that the apprenticeship might be abolished; on the ground that the planters had violated the contract; that they did not use the system as a preparation for freedom, but for purposes of continued oppression. The result of these combined influences was that the field-laborers were not held in apprenticeship till 1840, but were entirely emancipated, with the household slaves, on the first day of August, 1838. Rev. James Phillippo, Baptist Missionary in Jamaica, thus describes the day: "On the preceding evening, the missionary stations throughout the island were crowded with people, filling all the places of worship. They remained at their devotions till the day of liberty dawned, when they saluted it with joyous acclamations. Then they dispersed through the towns and villages, singing 'God save the queen' and rending the air with their shouts: 'Freedom's come!' 'We're free! We're free!' 'Our wives and children are free!' During the day, the places of worship were crowded to suffocation. The scenes presented exceeded all description. Joyous excitement pervaded the whole island. At Spanish Town, the Governor, Sir Lionel Smith, addressed the emancipated people, who formed a procession of 7,000, and escorted the children of the schools, about 2,000 in number, to the Government House. They bore banners and flags with various inscriptions, of which the following are samples. 'Education. Religion, and Social Order.' 'August First, 1838; the Day of our Freedom.' 'Truth and Justice have at last prevailed.' The children sang before the Government House, and His Excellency made a speech characterized by simplicity and affection, which was received with enthusiastic cheers. The procession then escorted their pastor to his house. In front of the Baptist Chapel were three triumphal arches, decorated with leaves and flowers, and surmounted by flags, bearing the inscriptions, 'Freedom has come!' 'Slavery is no more!' 'The chains are broken, Africa is free!' The enthusiasm of the multitude was wound up to the highest pitch. They wanted to greet all the flags; many of which bore the names of their benefactors, 'Sturge,' 'Brougham,' 'Sligo,' etc. The flags were unfurled, and for nearly an hour the air rang with exulting shouts, in which the shrill voices of the 2,000 children joined: 'We're free! We're free!' 'Our wives and our children are free!'"

Several of the kindly disposed planters gave rural fêtes to the laborers.* Long tables were spread in the lawns; arches of evergreens were festooned with flowers; and on the trees floated banners, bearing the names of those who had been most conspicuous in bringing about this blessed result. Songs were sung, speeches made, prayers offered, and a plentiful repast eaten. Mr. Phillippo says: "The conduct of the newly emancipated peasantry would have done credit to Christians of the most civilized country in the world. They were clean in their persons, and neat in their attire. Their behavior was modest, unassuming, and decorous in a high degree. There was no crowding, no vulgar familiarity, but all were courteous and obliging to each other, as members of one harmonious family. There was no dancing, gambling, or carousing. All seemed to have a sense of the obligations they owed to their masters, to each other, and to the civil authorities. The masters who were present at these fêtes congratulated their former dependents on the boon they had received, and hopes were mutually expressed that all past differences and wrongs might be forgiven. Harmony and cheerfulness smiled on every countenance; and the demon of discord disappeared, for a season. On some of the estates where these festivals were held, the laborers, with few individual exceptions, went to work as usual on the following day. *Many of them gave their first week of free labor as an offering of good-will to their masters.* Thus the period, from which many of the planters had apprehended the worst consequences, passed away in peace and harmony. Not a single instance of violence or insubordination, of serious disagreement or of intemperance, occurred in any part of the island."

After this safe transition to a better state of things, the public were informed of no troubles in Jamaica for several years, except deficiency of labor, and diminished production of sugar. Pro-slavery presses, both in England and America, eagerly proclaimed these deficiencies as the results of emancipation. But enough has been already said to prove, to any candid and reflecting mind, that these effects were attributable to other causes. *First.* Emancipation found nearly all the estates on the island heavily mortgaged; most of them for more than they were worth. The compensation money, received from the British government, was soon swallowed up, the planters hardly knew how. It helped them to pay off a portion of their long-accumulating arrears, but left them still involved in pecuniary difficulties. Many of them had not money to pay for labor; and some, who had it, retained too much of the spirit of slave-holding to be scrupulous about paying the negroes for their work.

Rev. Mr. Bleby says: "I know hundreds of colored laborers in Jamaica, who labored on the sugar plantations, and were defrauded of their wages. I knew a man who had a salary of one thousand pounds ($4,845) from an office under government, who employed two or three hundred laborers several months, then took the benefit of the Insolvent Act, and never paid them a cent. One of those great planting attorneys, who had fifty or sixty estates under his management, boasted to a friend of mine, that he made them profitable, by cheating the laborers out of half their wages, by one method or another. Is it surprising that the colored people should prefer to raise produce on a few acres of their own, to working on the plantations without wages? I was in Kingston when the railroad was made. It was done entirely by the colored people. The manager told me he could not desire laborers to work better. And what was the reason? Every Saturday night he paid them their wages."

Second. The tenure by which land was held was very precarious, as has already been explained by Governor Hincks. Planters in such a perverse state of mind as many were in Jamaica, were, of course, not slow to avail themselves of this instrument of oppression. When the emancipated laborers hired a hut and a bit of land on the estates where they had been accustomed to work, they were required to pay rent several times over. According to the statement of the Rev. Mr. Bleby, "The employer, would say to the husband, 'You must pay in labor, for the rent of your house.' Then he would say the same to the wife; and perhaps to other adult members of the family. Thus they manageed to get rent paid twice, and sometimes four times over." If the tenant expressed dissatisfaction, or gave offence in any way, or if his capricious landlord merely wanted to make him feel that he was still in his power, he was ejected at once, and obliged to take for his crops whatever the despotic employer saw fit to value them at. Such tyrannical proceedings were common all over the island. If a majority of the planters had *intended* to drive the negroes away from their estates, and force them " to skulk in the woods and live upon yams," as they had predicted, they could not have adopted a policy better suited to their purpose. The negroes, notwithstanding their strong local attachments, were driven from the sugar estates by these persecutions; but they did far better than " skulk in the woods, and retrograde to barbarism," as I shall presently show.

Rev. Mr. Phillipo, writing in 1843, says: "The planters persisted in their designs, and, at last multitudes of laborers were compelled to sacrifice their feelings of attachment to their domiciles, and to establish themselves in freeholds of of their own. Hence, and from no other cause, arose those reports of insolence and idleness, so widely and perseveringly circulated against the peasantry. It is delightful to add that the injustice and impolicy of such conduct have now become generally manifest; so that the causes of mutual dissatisfaction are now, to a considerable extent, extinct."

An intelligent gentleman in St. Thomas said to Mr. Thome, "The planters have set their hearts upon the ruin of the island, and they will be sorely disappointed, if it shouldn't come." But this disappointment was in reserve for them, and no ingenuity of theirs could prevent it. As individuals, they suffered for their blind and narrow policy; but public prosperity began to move steadily onward.

The Lord Bishop of Jamaica, in a circular recommending the establishment of schools for the emancipated peasantry, dated November, 1838, makes the following statement: "The peaceable demeanor of the objects of our instruction, and their generally acknowledged good behavior, are the natural fruits of being made better acquainted with the saving truths of the gospel; and no stronger proof can be given of their desire to obtain this knowledge than the fact that their choice in fixing their settlements is often influenced by the opportunities afforded for acquiring moral and religious instruction for themselves and their children."

Early in 1839, Sir Lionel Smith, Governor of the island, made the following statement, in an official document: " I have sent numerous testimonies to England, to show that where labor has been encouraged by fair remuneration and kind treatment, it has nowhere been wanting."

A part of the outcry concerning want of labor, and the depreciation of property arose from managers and attorneys, who conducted affairs for absentee proprietors. They wanted to buy estates themselves, at a low price; therefore, they irritated and discouraged the laborers, with the intention of driving them from the estates; and in some cases, they burned the sugar cane after it was gathered; giving as a reason that, from scarcity of labor, they could not convert it into sugar, except at prices which would entail a loss. The statements of such interested and unprincipled men were eagerly republished by pro-slavery papers in England and America; but, in this country, it was impossible for friends of freedom to procure any extensive republication of such testimony as the following, from the Rev. D. S. Ingraham, pastor of a church near Kingston, Jamaica, who visited the United States in 1840, and gave the following written testimony for publication: "Emancipation has greatly improved the value of all kinds of property. Land near my residence, which sold for fifteen dollars an acre a short time before emancipation, has been sold recently for sixty dollars an acre; and had there been ten times as much for sale, it would have sold readily for that price. I know of much land that now *leases* for more money in one year, than it would have *sold* for under slavery. Peace and safety have been promoted by emancipation. It was formerly thought necessary to have six regiments of soldiers, to keep the slaves in subjection, and also for the militia to meet monthly in each parish. Since freedom was declared, half of the soldiers have been removed; and where I live, the militia have entirely ceased to muster.* Emancipation has diminished crime. Jails formerly well filled, and often crowded, now have few tenants. A part of the house of correction in my parish is converted into a hospital, and the bloody old treadmill is incrusted with rust. Emancipation has promoted industry. A gentleman, who has been a planter in Jamaica for twenty years, told me there was undoubtedly far more work done in the island now than ever before. Indeed, any one can see that such is the case. Wherever you look, you see the forests giving place to gardens and cornfields, and numbers of comfortable houses growing up under the hand

---

* During slavery, the military defence of the West Indies annually cost England £2,000,000 ($9,960,000). For the single insurrection of 1832, in Jamaica, it cost the government $800,000; and private property was destroyed, to the amount of $6,000,000.

of industry and perseverance. Many villages have been built up entirely since freedom by those who were formerly slaves. A spirit of improvement has been called forth. Roads and streets are being McAdamized; there are many new markets in different parts of the country. Agricultural Societies are forming; and ploughs are coming into use. An overseer lately told me that he now ploughed upland for canes at one dollar and seventy-five cents per acre, instead of paying fifteen dollars an acre, to have it dug up, as formerly. There is a universal desire for knowledge among the emancipated people. They often send twenty miles in search of a preacher, or teacher. They have come to me and pleaded with an eloquence that no Christian could resist, saying: 'Minister, *do* come and sée we! We all ignorant; and so much big pickaniny, that don't know nothing. *Do* try for get we a teacher! We will take care of him.'"

Joseph J. Gurney, who visited Jamaica in 1840, says: " The imports of the island are rapidly increasing; trade improving; towns thriving; new villages rising up in every direction; property is much enhanced in value; well-managed estates are productive and profitable; expenses of management diminished; short methods of labor adopted; provisions cultivated on a larger scale than ever; and the people, wherever they are properly treated, are industrious, contented, and gradually accumulating wealth. Above all, the morals of the community are improving, and education is rapidly spreading.

" Under slavery, two hundred slaves were supported on the Papine estate; it is now worked by forty-three laborers. The estate of Halberstadt used to support one hundred and seventy slaves; now fifty-four laborers do all the work required. The support of the slaves on this estate cost £850 annually; the annual wages of the free laborers amount to £607 10*s*. 3*d*.

"' Do you see that excellent new stone wall round the field below us?' said a young physician. 'The necessary labor could not have been hired under slavery, or the apprenticeship, at less than thirteen dollars per chain; under freedom it cost only four dollars per chain. Still more remarkable is the fact that the whole of it was built, under the stimulus of job-work, by an invalid negro, who, under slavery, had been given up to total inaction.' Such was the fresh blood infused into the veins of this decrepit person by the genial hand of freedom, that he had executed a noble work, greatly improved his master's property, and realized for himself a handsome sum of money."

Dr. Stewart said to Mr. Gurney, " I believe, in my conscience, that property in Jamaica, *without* the slaves, is as valuable as it formerly was *with* them; and I believe its value would be doubled by sincerely turning away from all relics of slavery to the honest free working of a free system."

A despatch from Sir Charles Metcalfe, read in the House of Commons, 1842, declares : " The present condition of the peasantry of Jamaica is very striking. They are much improved in their habits, and are generally well-ordered and free from crime. They subscribe for their respective churches, and are constant in their attendance on divine worship, wearing good clothes, and many of them riding on horses. They send their children to school, and pay for their schooling." " It appears wonderful how so much has been accomplished in the island, in building, planting, digging, and making fences. The number of freeholders, who have become freeholders by their own industry and accumulation, amounted in 1840 to 7,340."

The *Jamaica Morning Journal* in February, 1843, says : " It is gratifying to observe the impetus which has been given to agricultural and literary societies. We do not recollect ever to have seen such vigorous efforts put forth for the improvement of the people and of agriculture, as have been within the last few months."

Rev. Mr. Phillippo, writing in the same year, says : " The term indolent can only be applied to the black population in the absence of remunerating employment; and even then they work on their own provision-grounds. Jamaica peasants are seldom seen lounging about, loitering along the roads, or spending their money at taverns and other similar places of resort. As for the great bulk of the people, making allowance for climate, no peasantry in the world can display more cheerful and persevering industry. In the time of slavery, unrestrained licentiousness was the order of the day. Every estate and every negro hut was a brothel. Now, marriage is the rule and concubinage the exception. Although every trifling infraction of the laws (contrary to former usage) is now publicly known and punished by magistrates, empty jails, and the absence of serious offences from the calendar of the courts, are sufficient evidence of the general decrease of crime."

The *Jamaica Morning Journal,* March, 1843, says: " Our readers will be surprised and pleased to learn that for the last five days not a single prisoner has been committed to the cage in this city [Kingston]. We record this fact with great pleasure, as we believe such a circumstance never before occurred since the building of the city."

Rev. Mr. Bleby says : " Before I left Jamaica (which was previous to 1848), no less than 50,000 colored people had become freeholders, as the fruit of their own industry. We are told these people will not work. How did they obtain these freeholds then? Some of them have mahogany bedsteads and side-boards in their houses. How do they get such furniture, except as the result of their own toil?"

JAMAICA AFTER 1846.

Now we are coming upon sad times. It has been stated that the West Indies had the monopoly of sugar in the British market, at an immense cost to the consumers. This had frequently called out remonstrances from the British people ; and in 1846 government repealed the tariff, which excluded other countries from competition. The result was a sudden and great fall in the price of sugar. " In 1840, sugar sold in bond at 49s. a cwt. ($11.86.) In 1848, it had sunk to 23s. 5d. ($5.65.") The result was many millions of dollars less in the receipts for their crops; and that was far from being the worst feature in the case. Business in the West Indies had for generations been carried on upon credit; and now credit was gone. The writer in the *Edinburgh* thus states the case : " The vast capital requisite for the production of sugar had been annually advanced by merchants in London, on the security of the crops. But, of course, when it was known that sugar had fallen so enormously in value, the merchants took fright, and the credit of the planter was gone. He was embarked in transactions on which a vast capital had been laid out, and which required a vast capital to carry them on; and capital he could not obtain." The suffering was dreadful. Thousands of families accustomed to the luxuries of wealth were reduced to poverty, without any of the habits that would have enabled them to bear it bravely. Their cry of distress resounded through the world. Pro-slavery presses in England and America exultingly proclaimed, "Behold the effects of emancipation?" and people without examining the subject, echoed the railing accusation. But one very important circumstance was overlooked; viz., that when this cry of distress arose, *slavery had been abolished fourteen years, and the apprenticeship had been abolished ten years.* By a little examination they might have ascertained that, previous to the repeal of the tariff, things were going on prosperously in the West Indies; which is sufficiently indicated by the fact that just before the blow came, they had been making an outlay to produce larger crops; a circumstance which rendered the blow all the heavier. Even Jamaica, with all her wretched mismanagement and financial disorders, was *beginning* to be prosperous, in consequence of emancipation, as we have shown.

Of the fall of property, subsequent to the repeal of the tariff some estimate may be formed from the following item. In 1838, the La Grange estate was sold for £25,000 ($121,125); and in 1840 the Windsor Forest estate sold for £40,000 ($193,800). In 1850, both those estates sold together for £11,000 ($53,295).

Mr. Bigelow, of the *New York Evening Post*, who visited Jamaica in 1850, says: "It is difficult to exaggerate, and still more difficult to define the poverty and industrial prostration of Jamaica. The natural wealth and spontaneous productiveness of the island are so great, that no one can starve, and yet it seems as if the faculty of accumulation were suspended. The productive power of the soil is running to waste; the finest land in the world may be had almost for the asking; labor receives no compensation; and the product of labor does not seem to know the way to market."

The soil still continued to be owned chiefly by absentees; an unincumbered estate of any size or value was hardly to be found; and since the depreciation of property, it was impossible to borrow money, to any considerable extent, on Jamaica estates.

Mr. Bigelow informs us that " Jamaica imports, annually, 70,000 barrels of flour; 90,000 bushels of corn; 300,000 pounds of tobacco; and 10 or 12,000,000 feet of lumber and sawed stuff. They have magnificent forests, but not a sawmill on the island. Even their bricks they import. They pay extravagant prices for articles, which could be cultivated in Jamaica with the utmost ease and abundance. Butter is $37\frac{1}{2}$ cts. a pound; milk $18\frac{3}{4}$ cts. a quart; flour from sixteen to eighteen dollars a barrel; etc. Nothing apparently can be more unnatural than for the people of this island, in their present poverty-stricken condition, to be paying such prices for daily food; yet nothing is more inevitable, so long as the land is held in such large quantities, and by absentee landlords. Till recently, such a thing was never known as a small farm of fifty or a hundred acres to be put under culture for profit."

As the planters and their advocates were continually complaining that wages were ruinously high, Mr. Bigelow made it a subject of special inquiry. He says: " To my utter surprise, I learned that the wages of men on the sugar and coffee plantations ranged from eighteen to twenty-four cents a day; and proportionably less for women and children. Out of these wages the laborers have *to board themselves.* Now, when it is considered that flour is eighteen dollars a barrel, eggs from three to five cents a piece, and ham twenty-five cents a pound, does not this cry of high wages appear absurd? Was the wolf's complaint of the lamb, for muddying the stream below him, more unreasonable? Are wages lower in any quarter of the civilized world? Four-fifths of all the grain consumed in Jamaica is grown in the United States, on fields where labor costs more than four times this price, and where every kind of provision, except fruit, is less expensive. The fact is, the negro cannot live on such wages, unless he ekes them out by stealing, or owns a lot of three or five acres. He is driven by necessity to purchase land and cultivate it for himself. He finds such labor so much better rewarded than that he bestows on the lands of others, that he naturally takes care of his own first, and gives his leisure to the properties of others.

"Of course, it requires no little energy and self-denial for a negro, upon such wages, to lay up enough to purchase a little estate; but if he does get one, he never parts with it, except for a larger or better one. I was greatly surprised to find the number of these colored proprietors already considerably over 100,000, and continually increasing. When one reflects that only sixteen years ago there was scarcely a colored landholder on the island, it is unnecessary to say that this class of the population appreciate the privileges of free labor and a homestead far more correctly than might be expected; more especially when it is borne in mind that seven-tenths of them were born in slavery, and spent many years as bondmen. Their properties average, I should think, about three acres. They have a direct interest in cultivating them economically and intelligently. The practice of planning their own labor, encouraged by the privilege of reaping its rewards, exerts upon them the most important educational influence; the results of which will soon be much more apparent than they now are."

Pro-slavery writers declare that these negro farmers have not raised five pounds of sugar a year for exportation. But does that prove they are lazy? Where butter is 37½ cts. a pound, eggs from three to five cents a piece, onions 12½ cts. a pound, and other provisions at the same rate, they can turn their land to better account, than to enter into competition with sugar makers. When the same system is introduced that Gov. Hincks mentions in Barbadoes, they will doubtless turn their attention to raising sugar canes.

There is much evidence that there is no actual want of labor in Jamaica, though it has doubtless been alienated from the large sugar plantations. Firstly, by the harsh and unjust treatment of many of the planters. Secondly, by the state of bankruptcy in which emancipation found them, and which rendered them unable to pay for work. Thirdly, and probably the strongest cause for all, was the inability of the laborers to hire land on their estates, with any degree of security. Mr. Charles Tappan, of Boston, who visited Jamaica in 1858, says: "The alleged want of labor is a false cry. Where labor is said to be deficient, it can be traced to causes within the planters' control to remove. Of these, insufficient wages, unpunctual payment of the same, or no payment at all, are stated to be the chief." "In conversing with planters, I learned that laborers can easily be obtained for a fair compensation and kind treatment. But it is a fact that the emancipated much prefer to work on their own few acres of land." Mr. S. B. Slack, an old native resident of Jamaica, writes thus to Mr. Tappan in 1858: "With few exceptions the planters now acknowledge that emancipation was a blessing. Some soreness was felt at the commencement; and it was manifested in the injudicious acts of ejecting laborers from the cottages they had occupied since infancy, and destroying their provision-grounds, which led them to purchase freeholds of their own, and thus become independent of their labor on the estates. But if the negroes are as lazy as they are represented, how is it that in the construction of a new road across the island more laborers can be obtained than are required? How is it that the Water Works Company are sure to have competitors for employment? How does it happen that the Railway Company are equally well off for labor? The answer is, because the laborers are liberally and punctually paid; and they are willing to work, when they are sure to obtain the reward."

Sir Charles Grey, who was Governor of Jamaica, in 1850, says: "There are few races of men who will work harder, or more perseveringly, than the negroes, when they are sure of getting the produce of their labor."

The Free Villages, which have sprung up since emancipation are described by all travellers as a new and most pleasing feature in the scenery of the West Indies. In the days of slavery, laborers generally lived in thatched hovels, with mud walls, thrown together without any order or arrangement. A few calabashes, a water jar, and a mortar for pounding corn, mainly constituted their furniture. As the women were driven into the fields to toil early and late, they had no time for household cleanliness. These negro dwellings looked picturesque in the distance, nestling among palm-trees and tamarind groves; but, like slavery itself, they would not bear a close inspection. As you came near them, the senses were offended by decaying vegetables, and nauseous effluvia. Now, the laborers live in Free Villages, regularly laid out. The houses are small, many of them, built of stone or wood, with shingled roofs, green blinds, and verandahs, to shield them from the sun. Most of them are neatly thatched, and generally plastered and whitewashed outside and in. They now have looking-glasses, chairs, and side-boards decorated with pretty articles of glass and crockery. Each dwelling has its little plot of vegetables, generally neatly kept, and many of them have flower-gardens in front, glowing with all the bright hues of the tropics. In 1843, Mr. Phillippo said that, by a rough estimate, the number of these villages in Jamaica was about two hundred, and the number of acres of land purchased was not less than 100,000. It was estimated that in the course of four years, the emancipated apprentices had paid £170,000 ($823,650) for land and buildings. And that was done when wages were from eighteen to twenty-four cents a day, out of which they boarded themselves! And these were the people who, the slave-holders were so sure would "skulk in the woods, and live on yams," rather than work, after they ceased to be flogged!

The names of these villages give pleasant indication of the gratitude of the colored people toward their benefactors. They are called Clarkson, Wilberforce, Buxton, Brougham, Macaulay, Thompson, Gurney, Sligo, etc. The names given to their own little homes have almost a poetic interest, so touching and expressive is their simplicity. The following are samples : " Happy Retreat;" " Thank God for it;" " A Little of my Own;" " Liberty and Content;" " Thankful Hill;" " Come and See."

Joseph J. Gurney visited Clarkson Town in the winter of 1839, and has recorded that he was "delighted with its appearance, and with the manners, intelligence, and hospitality of the people." Mr. Phillippo, who was familiar with these villages, says : "The groups often presented are worthy of the painter's pencil, or the poet's song. Amid the stillness of a Sabbath evening, many families, after their return from the house of God, may be seen gathered together in the shadow of the trees, which overhang their cottages, singing hymns, or listening to the reading of the Scriptures, with none to molest or make them afraid."

Mr. Charles Tappan says: "On landing at Kingston, I must confess I was half inclined to believe the story so industriously circulated, that the emancipated slave is more idle and vicious than any other of God's intelligent creatures; but when I rode through the valleys and over the mountains, and found everywhere an industrious, sober people, I concluded all the vagabonds of the island had moved to the sea-shore, to pick up a precarious living by carrying baggage, begging, etc.; and such, upon inquiry, I found to be the fact. Wherever I went in the rural districts, I found contented men and women, cultivating sugar cane, and numerous vegetables and fruits, on their own account. Their neat, well-furnished cottages compared well with the dwellings of pioneers in our own country. I found in them mahogany furniture, crockery and glass ware, and shelves of useful books. I saw Africans, of unmixed blood, grinding their own sugar cane in their own mills, and making their own sugar. I attended a large meeting called to decide the question about inviting a schoolmaster to settle among them. There was only one man who doubted the expediency of taking the children from work and sending them to school. One said: 'My little learning enabled me to see that a note, given to me in payment for a horse, was not written according to contract.' Another said: 'I should have been wronged out of forty pounds of coffee I sold in Kingston, the other day, if I hadn't known how to cipher.' Another said: 'I shall not have much property to leave my children, but if they have learning, they can get property.' Another said: 'Those that can read will be more likely to get religion.' All these people had been slaves, or were the children of slaves. I saw no intoxicated person in Jamaica; and when it is considered that every man there can make rum, it strikes me as very remarkable."

Here we have the germ of that middling class, which is the best reliance in every community, and which can never co-exist with slavery.

The fall of sugar as we have said prostrated the West Indies for a time; and no Colony was so badly situated to sustain it as Jamaica, with her overwhelming debts, her wretched management, her financial disorders, and her laborers alienated from the sugar estates by persistence in treating freemen as if they were slaves. Lord Sligo stated, in an official report, that many of the planters threw estates out of cultivation in 1832, because they were so sure that the negroes would not work after the Act of Emancipation had passed. Then, when the fall of sugar came in 1847 a great many planters were obliged to abandon their estates, from inability to borrow money to carry them on. Mr. Bigelow states that, in 1850, there were 400,000 acres of sugar and coffee plantations abandoned to weeds and underbush.

But there is a recuperative power in Free Trade, as there is in Free Labor. The West Indies soon began to rise from the severe but temporary pressure, occasioned by the repeal of the Tariff. In some cases property passed out of the fettered hands of bankrupts to those, who being unincumbered, could take a fair start; while some of the old proprietors learned wisdom from experience, and managed more judiciously. Even Jamaica is coming in for her share in these beneficial changes. That her waste places are beginning to be restored is indicated by the following article from the *Kingston Morning Journal*, 1857 : " On Monday last, the roads leading to Great Valley estate presented a lively appearance. Men and women, old and young, strong and weak, were all hastening toward a common point of attraction. Gaudy handkerchiefs were flying from flag-poles, the people were singing and dancing, and every thing gave token of a day much honored by the peasantry. It was no wedding or merry-making. They were in working-clothes, with hoes and pickaxes on their shoulders. From every track and by-path came individuals to increase the crowd. All seemed happy and in haste. All were sweeping toward the gate of the Great Valley works. We said to an old man, whose head was white with the frost of eighty winters : 'Hallo! where are all these people going?' Taking off his cap, he answered, 'Me good buckra, me neber expect to see him Great Valley da rise. Him goin' for 'tablish cane; make sugar agin. Good for we all. Eberybody for help.' ' But you are too old to do any thing.' ' Da true, me massa. Me no hab trong. But me must do someting. Me fetch water. Me heart trong, do me han' weak.' To another we said : ' Where are you taking that cart-load of cane-tops to, my man?' 'To the Great Valley, sir. They are going to establish the sugar estate again; and I am carrying them all the cane-tops I have, to plant.' We said to a woman with a great bundle of cane-tops on her head, 'Are you going to the Great Valley, too?' 'Yes, sir. It's a great day for us all. Everybody must help.' To another, who headed a group of seventy or eighty children, we said, 'Where are you going, my friend?' 'I am the master of Pondside school, sir. The girls and boys all begged a holiday, to carry cane-tops to the Great Valley, and help them dig cane-holes. A new proprietor has bought the estate, and everybody wants to help him.' 'But don't you think there will be difficulty in procuring labor?' 'No, sir, not a bit; if the people are treated honestly and kindly. The new proprietor has a kindly way with him, and treats the people encouragingly; and a kind word goes a great way with our people. But I must follow my scholars. You can hear by their noise that they have already joined the digging party, there where the flags are flying.' And sure enough the ringing sound of children's shouts and laughter was borne joyously on the breeze.

"Great Valley is a noble estate of 4,000 acres, pleasantly situated between hills. It was formerly considered the second estate in the parish of Hanover. Now the works looked like some venerable ruin. Windows broken, chimneys tumbling, roofs falling in, lightning-rod swinging to and fro, carts and trucks rotting in the middle of the yard, the noble tank filled up with weeds, among which wild ducks were floating. But these ruined walls are to be rebuilt. The solitary places, now musty with mould and decay, will soon be filled with a busy throng, and the pleasant perfume of sugar-boiling will replace the unwholesome vapors. It is a pleasant prospect; and seems an omen of more prosperous days for our Island of Jamaica."

Between 1853 and 1855, there was an increase in exports to the amount of £166,049 ($804,507.40).

The Governor, in his report for 1855, says: "I feel more confident of the ultimate restoration of prosperity than I ever did before."

The Governor, in his speech at the opening of the Legislature, 1858, says: "A still progressive increase, both in the quantity of the staple exports, and in the amount of revenue derived from duties on articles of consumption, indicate a gradual improvement in the productive industry of the Colony." He alludes to a succession of dry seasons, that have diminished the crops; and yet with that very serious drawback, the exports were increasing. He admits that complaints still came from the old plantations of a deficiency of continuous labor; which he says he can readily believe, from the "admitted fact that the portion of the agricultural peasantry, who, with their families, industriously and systematically apply themselves to the independent production of sugar, and other staples, is day by day increasing."

When Lord Belmore, the Governor in 1832, said to the Jamaica Assembly, "Depend upon it, gentlemen, the resources of this fine island will never be fully developed, until slavery is abolished," he gave them very great offence. The grandsons of the men he offended will see his prediction verified. Even amid all the desolation and discouragement in 1850, Mr. Bigelow says: "I made extensive inquiry, but I did not find a man upon the island who regretted the Emancipation Act, or who, if I may take their own professions, would have restored slavery, if it had been in their power."

Ernst Noel, who writes from Jamaica to the *New York Times*, in the winter of 1860, says: "It is an undoubted fact that the exportation of coffee in Jamaica has declined from twenty-five and thirty millions to five and six millions; but it is also an undoubted fact that where one pound was used in the island prior to emancipation ten are used now. [Every laborer has his cup of coffee now.] It is my firm conviction that there is no such great discrepancy between the amount *grown* at the time of emancipation, and the amount now grown; especially when the extent of *exhausted* coffee land is taken into account. The same statement will apply with much greater force to provisions of every description. It is undoubtedly true that most of the large coffee properties formerly in cultivation have been abandoned, or turned to other uses. Coffee requires new land; and the clearance of fifty acres of wood is a Herculean enterprise for coffee planters, among whom want of *capital* prevails as much as among sugar planters. But whatever *large* coffee planters may say about their profits and losses, it is a notorious fact that thousands and thousands of settlers grow the delicious berry to advantage; as any merchant engaged in the trade will be able to testify. They come to the towns and villages with one, two, six, or a dozen bags, and in this way many a cargo is made up for foreign ports."

The same writer says that several experienced planters, to whom he proposed questions concerning investment of capital in that island, assured him that profits from ten to twenty per cent might be securely counted upon.

NOTE. — In Mauritius, a fertile island in the Indian Ocean, belonging to Great Britain, the sugar crop, during the last ten years of slavery, averaged 68,741,120 lbs. annually. During four years, after emancipation, beginning with 1845, the average crop was 171,122,500 lbs.; an increase of 102 millions of pounds annually; nearly 150 per cent in favor of free labor.

CHAPTER VI.

EMANCIPATION SAFE IN EVERY INSTANCE

" Right *never* comes wrong."
— *Old Maxim.*

WHENEVER immediate emancipation is urged, the "horrors of St. Domingo" are always brought forward to prove it dangerous. This is one of numerous misstatements originating in prejudice, and afterward taken for granted by those who have not examined the subject. The first troubles between the white and black races in St. Domingo were the result of oppressive and unlawful treatment of the free colored population, who were numerous, and many of them wealthy proprietors. The whites were determined to wrest from them certain rights which the French government had secured to them. The next troubles were occasioned by an attempt to *restore slavery*, after it had been for some years abolished. It was never the *granting* of rights to the colored people that produced bloodshed or disturbance. All the disasters to the whites came in consequence of *withholding* those rights, in the first instance, and afterward from a forcible attempt to *take them away*, after they had long been peacefully and prosperously enjoyed under the protection of French laws.

In 1793, the National Assembly proclaimed liberty to all slaves under the dominion of France; more than 600,000 in number; and history shows that the measure proved safe. *In St. Domingo emancipation was both peaceful and prosperous in its results.* Col. Malenfant, a slave-holder resident in the island at the time, published "A Historical and Political Memoir of the Colonies," in which he says: "After this public act of emancipation the negroes remained quiet, both in the south and west. There were estates which had neither owners nor managers upon them; yet upon those estates, though abandoned, the negroes continued their labors, where there were any of the inferior agents left to guide them; and where there was no white man, in any capacity, to take direction of affairs, they betook themselves to planting provisions. Several of my neighbors, proprietors or managers, were in prison; and the negroes on their plantations were in the habit of coming to me to direct them in their work. If you will take care not to talk to them of the restoration of slavery, but to talk to them of freedom, you may with that word chain them to their labor. In the plain of the Cul de Sac, on the plantation Gouraud, I managed four hundred and fifty laborers for more than eight months after liberty had been granted them. Not one of them refused to work. Yet that plantation was reputed to have been under the worst discipline, and the slaves the most idle of any in the plain. I inspired the same activity into three other plantations, of which I had the management. Ninety-nine out of a hundred blacks are perfectly well aware that labor is the process by which they can obtain means to gratify their wants and their tastes; and therefore they are desirous to work." In describing the latter part of 1796, Col. Malenfant says: "The Colony is flourishing. The whites live peacefully and happily upon their estates, and the negroes continue to work for them." Gen. Lecroix, who published "Memoirs for a History of St. Domingo," speaks of wonderful progress in agriculture in 1797. He says: "The Colony marched, as by enchantment, toward its ancient splendor; cultivation prospered, and every day furnished perceptible proofs of progress."

SUCH WAS THE EFFECT OF EMANCIPATION IN ST. DOMINGO!

In 1801, Gen. Vincent, a proprietor of estates in St. Domingo, went to France to lay before the government the plan of a new Constitution for the island. He found Napoleon Bonaparte, then First Consul, preparing to send out an armament to restore slavery in St. Domingo. General Vincent earnestly remonstrated against the expedition. He assured the Consul that the negroes were orderly and industrious, and that every thing was going on peacefully and prosperously for all parties; that it was unnecessary, and therefore cruel, to attempt to reverse this happy state of things. But there was a class of old despotic planters who clamored for the restoration of the arbitrary power, which they had most cruelly abused. Unfortunately, Bonaparte considered it good policy to conciliate that class; and he persisted in his purpose. He tried to *restore slavery*, by military force, and the consequence was that the French were driven out of the island, with great bloodshed.

In Guadaloupe, where liberty was proclaimed at the same time as in St. Domingo, the sudden transition took place with perfect safety. The reports from the Governors, for successive years, bear testimony that the emancipated laborers were universally industrious and submissive to the laws.

Gen. Lafayette, the consistent friend of human freedom, made a practical experiment of emancipation, as early as 1785. In the French Colony of Cayenne, most of the soil belonged to the crown, and he was able to obtain it on easy terms. He expended $30,000 in purchasing land and slaves.* He employed an amiable and judicious gentleman to take the management. The first thing the agent did, when he arrived in Cayenne, was to call the slaves together, and in their presence burn all the whips and other instruments of punishment. He informed them that their owner, Gen. Lafayette had bought them for the purpose of enabling them to obtain their freedom. He then stated to them the laws and regulations by which the estate would be governed, and the pecuniary advantages that would be granted, according to degrees of industry. This stimulus operated like a charm. The energy of the laborers redoubled, and they were obedient to the wishes of their manager. He died from the effects of the climate.* But when the slaves in all the French Colonies were emancipated in 1793, the laborers on this estate in Cayenne waited upon the new agent, and said if the land still belonged to Gen. Lafayette they wished to resume their labor for him on the old terms, giving as a reason that they were "desirous to promote the interests of one who had treated them like men, and cheered their toil by making it a certain means of freedom."

In 1811 the British authorities emancipated all the slaves in Java. This also proved a complete success; as any one can ascertain by examining the account given by Sir Stamford Rafiles, who was Governor of the island.

At successive periods, between 1816 and 1828, the South American Republics, Buenos Ayres, Chili, Bolivia, Peru, Colombia and Guatemala emancipated all their slaves. In some of those States means were taken for the instruction of young slaves, who were enfranchised on arriving at a certain age. In other States, slaves of all ages were emancipated after a certain date, fixed by law. In no one instance were these changes productive of any injury to life or property.

In 1828 the British government emancipated all the slaves in Cape Colony. 30,000 Hottentot Helots were admitted by law to all the rights and privileges of the white inhabitants. The slave-holders in the Colony remonstrated vehemently against this measure. They declared that the Hottentots were stupid, sensual, brutal, vicious, and totally incapable of taking care of themselves. They predicted awful outrages, as the consequence of emancipating a horde of such degraded wretches. But the event proved quite otherwise. The poor creatures were grateful for their freedom, and tried to behave as well as they knew how. All went on as peaceably as before, as concerned the white inhabitants, and much *more* peaceably, as concerned the blacks, who had previously suffered shocking barbarities at the hands of their masters. In the sunlight of freedom even the Hottentots have been gradually emerging out of barbarism. Year by year they pay more for British manufactures, because they wear calico and woollen cloth, instead of sheepskin mantles. They have horses and wagons, and flocks of their own, and their small weekly contributions to the Missionary Societies at the Cape amount to many hundreds of dollars.

From the time that Mexico became independent of Spain, in 1821, there was an increasing conviction in the public mind, that the existence of slavery was inconsistent with their professed principles as a Republic. This feeling soon manifested itself in laws. The prices of slaves were fixed by magistrates, and they were required to work, at stipulated wages, till they had paid for themselves. Protective laws were passed, enabling the servants to work for others, if they were not justly and humanely treated by their masters. Transfers of service might also take place to accommodate the masters; but never without consent of the servants. Mr. Ward, the British Minister to Mexico, in his work on that country, speaks very highly of the beneficial effects produced by these regulations. He says they gave a powerful stimulus to industry, and rapidly increased agricultural prosperity. A Mississippi slave-holder, who went to reside in Matamoras, was also so much pleased with the results of this experiment, that he wrote of it with enthusiasm, as an example highly important to the United States. He declared that the value of plantations was soon increased by the introduction of free labor. He says: "No one was made poor by it. It gave property to the servant, and increased the riches of the master." Free labor commended itself so much in this process, that on September 15th, 1829, President Guerrero published the following decree: "Being desirous to signalize the Anniversary of Mexican Independence by an act of national justice and beneficence, we hereby declare slavery forever abolished in this Republic. Consequently, all those individuals who, until this day, have been considered slaves, are free!" No interruption of public peace or prosperity followed this just decree.

In 1831, 3,000 prize negroes received freedom in South Africa; 400 in one day. No difficulty or disorder occurred. All gained homes; and at night scarcely an idler was to be seen.

In 1848, the French government, after careful examination into the state of things in the British West Indies, decreed immediate emancipation to all the slaves in their Colonies. M. Arago, formerly member of the Provisional Government, wrote thus, in 1851: "Much has been said of the ruin which the Act of Emancipation has scattered over our Colonies. But it should be remembered that *they were in a deplorable condition for a long time previous.* The Chamber of Deputies resounded daily with their lamentations. Extreme and utterly inadmissible measures for their *relief* were continually proposed. The Act of Emancipation cut peacefully one of the most complicated questions our social state afforded. Free labor has taken the place of slave labor without much resistance. So far, it has been attended with results sufficiently favorable, and these cannot fail to grow better." O. Lafayette, grandson of General Lafayette, member of the Chamber of Deputies, wrote thus, in 1851: "In one day, as by the stroke of a wand, 150,000 human beings were snatched from the degradation, in which they had been held by former legislation, and resumed their rank in the great human family. And this great event occurred without any of those disorders and struggles, which had been threatened, in order to perplex the consciences of the friends of abolition."

In 1841, the Bey of Tunis prohibited the exportation or importation of slaves, and declared all children free that should be born in his dominions after December 8th, 1842. In 1846, he proclaimed that slavery was abolished entirely, "for the honor of God, and to distinguish man from the brute creation." To these measures he was greatly influenced by the British Minister, Sir Thomas Reade.

Not far from the same date, Sweden proclaimed emancipation in the Island of St. Bartholomew, the only place under her dominion where slavery existed.

Christian VIII. of Denmark, and his Queen, Caroline, were so openly in favor of emancipation, that the price of slaves in their dominions became greatly reduced. The kind-hearted Queen obtained a promise from the King that he would celebrate the anniversary of their Silver Wedding by a decree of universal emancipation. Accordingly, on the 28th of July, 1847, it was proclaimed that all children born on or after that day should be free; and that all the slaves in the Danish possessions, about 30,000 in number, should receive their freedom in 1859. This was intended to give time to prepare for the change; but it worked badly. It made the negroes restless to hear of freedom without obtaining it; and this feeling was increased by intercourse with the neighboring French islands, where all had been proclaimed unconditionally free. The masters were opposed to emancipation, and not at all disposed to conciliate their laborers. In July, 1848, local insurrections broke out. A good deal of property was destroyed, but few lives lost, except those of slaves who were executed. The panic produced caused a proclamation of immediate emancipation; since which there have been no insurrections, nor any fear of them. Fifty dollars for each slave was awarded to the masters, who have never ceased to grumble against the government and against the negroes. Such a transition, of course, could not take place without temporary evils and inconveniences. The effects of a system so bad as slavery cannot be suddenly outgrown, either by masters or servants. But improvement is more and more perceptible as years pass on. A gentleman writing from St. Thomas to the *N. Y. Tribune*, September, 1854, says: "The former owners are constantly complaining of the ignorance, faithlessness, and degradation of the negroes, without seeming to have any consciousness of the fact that they themselves have brought them to this very character and condition. Whether their state is *at once* bettered is not the decisive question, but whether they are in a condition where there is a chance for improvement. And for my own part, the respectability attained by many persons of color in this town, and the industry and capacity manifested by large numbers, in various employments, as artisans, clerks, bookkeepers, and public officials, give me a hope I never before entertained, of the certain advancement of the African race, wherever they shall become disembarrassed of the shackles of slavery, and of an unjust social prejudice."

A Boston gentleman, who visited Santa Cruz in the spring of 1859, writes thus: "You would be delighted with the effects of emancipation, as we see them all round us, with abundant opportunities to examine them. The pay which the Danish government has settled for voluntary labor sounds very low [five dollars a month]. But the artificial wants of the laborers are so few, and the necessaries of life are so easily supplied in this perpetual summer, that the thrifty and industrious have already succeeded in laying up enough to build comfortable little homes, and bring up their children to trades. The vice which had always been encouraged among them, for their masters' gain, carries its poison among them yet; but they are gradually acquiring a pride of matrimony. A noble young Episcopal minister is laboring unweariedly for their moral and intellectual elevation, almost unaided by the white population, who look coldly upon his labors. The progress made in two years has been surprising indeed."

In 1857, the Dutch abolished slavery in their West India

Colonies. The government paid a certain sum to the masters, and took the entire control of the slaves, who were to work till they repaid the sum advanced for their freedom. Children under five years were free at once, and moderate prices were fixed by law for all the slave population, graduated according to their ages. As soon as the stipulated price was offered by any slave, he became a freeman. Wages were also fixed by law; and in case any planters refused to submit to the prescribed regulations, rural settlements were formed where the colored people could find employment, under the superintendence of managers appointed by government, aided by colleagues who were elected by the laborers. Of course, the success of this experiment will greatly depend on the good-temper and good judgment of the men who manage it. I have no means of ascertaining the degree of financial prosperity in the Dutch West India Colonies since emancipation began to take effect; but I know that *before the abolition of slavery, they were complaining of "ruin" and begging for "relief."* The Colony of Surinam, *under slavery*, made this statement. "Out of nine hundred and seventeen, plantations, six hundred and thirty-six have been totally abandoned. Of the remainder, sixty-five grow nothing but wood and provisions." The small balance of estates not included in this description, were declared to be on the road to destruction. Whether free labor works better results, time will show. But one thing is already certain; the transition was made with perfect safety. In 1859, the Dutch abolished slavery in all their East India possessions; where it had existed under a comparatively mild form. There was one very remarkable and beautiful feature in this transaction. The government offered an assessed compensation to the masters; but *many of them refused to take it, while others took it and gave it to the emancipated slaves, who had worked so many years without wages.*

History proves that emancipation has *always* been safe. It is an undeniable fact, that not one white person has ever been killed, or wounded, or had life or property endangered by any violence attendant upon immediate emancipation, in any of the many cases where the experiment has been tried. On the contrary, it has always produced a feeling of security in the public mind.

CHAPTER VII.

CONCLUDING REMARKS.

I APPEAL to candid readers whether I have not, in the preceding pages, fairly made out a case in favor of immediate emancipation. I have not advanced opinions, or theories; I have simply stated facts. In view of these facts, is it not unjust and irrational to persist in calling immediate emancipation a "fanatical" idea? Leaving the obvious considerations of justice and humanity entirely out of the question, I ask whether experience has not proved it to be a measure of plain, practical good sense, and sound policy. The trouble in forming a correct estimate on this subject arises mainly from our proneness to forget that negroes are *men*, and, consequently, governed by the same laws of human nature, which govern all men. Compulsion always excites resistance; reward always stimulates exertion. Kindness has upon the human soul an influence as renovating as sunshine upon the earth; and no race is so much and so easily influenced by it as the negroes. Jamaica overseers, blinded by the long habit of considering slaves as cattle, said to them, after they became apprentices, "Work faster, you black rascal! or I'll flog you." That excited the apprentice to remind them they had no power to do it. The retort enraged the overseers; and the magistrate was called upon to punish the laborer for his insolence in expressing the feelings of a man. The Antigua planters acted with more enlightened policy. They wisely gave up their power into the hands of the law. If they chanced to see a laborer rather dilatory, they said, "We expect better things of *freemen:*" and that simple appeal to their manhood, we are told, invariably quickened their motions, while it gratified their feelings.

Free labor has so obviously the advantage, in all respects, over slave labor, that posterity will marvel to find in the history of the nineteenth century any record of a system so barbarous, so clumsy, and so wasteful. Let us make a very brief comparison. The slave is bought, sometimes at a very high price; in free labor there is no such investment of capital. The slave does not care how slowly or carelessly he works; it is the freeman's interest to do his work well and quickly. The slave is indifferent how many tools he spoils; the freeman has a motive to be careful. The slave's clothing is indeed very cheap, but it is provided by his master, and it is of no consequence to him how fast it is destroyed; the hired laborer pays more for his garments, but he has a motive for making them last six times as long. The slave contrives to spend as much time as he can in the hospital; the free laborer has no time to spare to be sick. Hopeless poverty and a sense of being unjustly dealt by, impels the slave to steal from his master, and he has no social standing to lose by indulging the impulse; with the freeman pride of character is a powerful inducement to be honest. A salary must be paid to an overseer to compel the slave to work; the freeman is impelled by a desire to increase his property, and add to the comforts of himself and family. We should question the sanity of a man who took the main-spring out of his watch, and hired a boy to turn the hands round. Yet he who takes from laborers the natural and healthy stimulus of wages, and attempts to supply its place by the driver's whip, pursues a course quite as irrational.

When immediate emancipation is proposed, those who think loosely are apt to say, " But would you turn the slaves loose upon society?" There is no sense in such a question. Emancipated slaves are restrained from crime by the same laws that restrain other men; and experience proves that a consciousness of being *protected* by legislation inspires them with *respect* for the laws.

But of all common questions, it seems to me the most absurd one is, " What would you *do* with the slaves, if they were emancipated?" There would be no occasion for doing *any* thing with them. Their labor is needed where they are; and if white people can get along with them, under all the disadvantages and dangers of slavery, what should hinder their getting along under a system that would make them work better and faster, while it took from them all motive to rebellion?

It is often asked. "What is your plan?" It is a very simple one: but it would prove as curative as the prophet's direction, "Go wash, and be clean." It is merely to stimulate laborers by wages, instead of driving them by the whip. When that plan is once adopted, education and religious teaching, and agricultural improvements will soon follow, as matters of course.

It is not to be supposed that the transition from slavery to freedom would be unattended with inconveniences. All changes in society involve some disadvantages, either to classes or individuals. Even the introduction of a valuable machine disturbs for a while the relations of labor and capital. But it is important to bear in mind that *whatever difficulties might attend emancipation would be slight and temporary; while the difficulties and dangers involved in the continuance of slavery are permanent, and constantly increasing.* Do you ask in what way it is to be accomplished? I answer, That must finally be decided by legislators. It is *my* business to use all my energies in creating the *will* to do it; because I know very well that "Where there is a *will* there is a *way*;" and I earnestly entreat all who wish well to their country to aid me in this work.

APPENDIX.

IN WHICH STATEMENTS ARE BROUGHT DOWN TO THE CLOSE OF 1860

Mr. Bigelow, of the *New York Evening Post*, whose book is often quoted in the preceding pages, testifies to the condition of the British West India Islands as late as 1850. Ten years later, Mr. William G. Sewell, of the *New York Times*, visited those Islands, and on his return published a book called, "THE ORDEAL OF FREE LABOR." It is written in a very candid spirit, and evinces careful observation. He has no disposition to conceal that temporary difficulties attend the transition from one system of labor to another; but he proves conclusively, that slavery brought increasing ruin, and freedom is bringing increasing prosperity. We subjoin a few brief extracts:

IMPORTS. "Between 1820 and 1834, British Guiana imported annually to the value of $3,700,000; in 1850, the imports of Guiana were valued at $5,660,000. The annual imports of Trinidad, between 1820 and 1834, averaged in value $1,500,000; in 1850, they were valued at $3,000,000. The annual imports of Barbadoes, during the same period, averaged in value $2,850,000; in 1850, they were valued at $4,660,000. The imports of Antigua, during the same period, averaged $600,000; in 1850, they were valued at $1,230,000. The total exhibit represents the annual import trade, before emancipation, as valued at $8,840,000; and valued at the present time at $14,600,000: or, *an excess of imports, under a free system, of the value of five millions, seven hundred and sixty thousand dollars.*"

EXPORTS. "For four years prior to emancipation, British Guiana exported an annual average of 98,000,000 lbs. of sugar; while from 1856 to 1860, its annual average export rose to 100,600,000 lbs. For four years prior to emancipation, Trinidad annually exported an average of 37,000,000 lbs. of sugar; while from 1856 to 1860, its annual average export rose to 62,000,000 lbs. Four years prior to emancipation, Barbadoes annually exported an average of 32,800,000 lbs. of sugar; from 1856 to 1860, its annual average export rose to 78,000,000 lbs. Four years prior to emancipation,

Antigua exported an annual average of 19,500,000 lbs. of sugar; from 1856 to 1860, its annual average export rose to 24,400,000 lbs. The total exhibit is 187,300,000 lbs. annually exported before emancipation, and 265,000,000 lbs. annually exported now; or, *an excess of exports, with free labor, of seventy-seven millions, seven hundred thousand pounds of sugar.*"

"In the exports, I have made mention of sugar only; but if all other articles of commerce be included, and a comparison be instituted between the import and export trade of Guiana, Trinidad, Barbadoes, and Antigua, under slavery, and their trade under freedom, *the annual balance in favor of freedom will be found to have reached already fifteen millions of dollars, at the very lowest estimate.*"

"The increase of imports is to be attributed to the improved condition and ampler means of the peasantry developed by the dawn of freedom."

EFFECTS OF FREEDOM ON THE LABORERS.

"In Barbadoes, within the last fifteen years, in spite of the extraordinary price of land and the low rate of wages, the small proprietors, holding less than five acres, have increased from 1100 to 3537. A great majority of them were formerly slaves. This fact speaks volumes. It is certainly an evidence of industrious habits, and is a remarkable contradiction to the prevailing idea that the negro will work only under compulsion. That idea was formed and fostered from the habits of the negro as a *slave.* His habits as a *free man,* developed under a wholesome stimulus and settled by time, are in striking contrast to his habits as a slave. None are more ready than the planters themselves to admit that the free laborer is a better, more cheerful, and more industrious workman, than the slave ever was under a system of compulsion. These are the opinions of men, who were themselves once violently opposed to freedom, and who still strive to keep the laboring classes in complete dependence; and they are opinions so universal that I have sought diligently, but in vain, to hear them contradicted."

"In St. Vincent, the returns for 1857 show that no less than 8209 persons were then living in their own houses, built by themselves since emancipation. Within the last twelve years, from ten to twelve thousand acres have been brought under cultivation by small proprietors, owning from one to five acres, and growing arrow-root, provisions, and minor articles for export. The statistical returns from which I gather these figures further state that *there are no paupers on the island.*"

"In Trinidad, there is, unquestionably, a certain amount of idleness and vagabondism among the Creole laborers; but I see no evidence that these vices exist in larger proportion among them, than they would exist among any other class of laborers similarly situated. In leaving the estates, the great majority were actuated by a desire to better their circumstances, and to lead a more independent life. Land was cheap and abundant, and they preferred to have their own property, rather than labor at low wages in a condition of precarious servitude. Added to this, the course of the planters contributed greatly to the very evil which they dreaded, and from which they afterward so severely suffered. Instead of endeavoring by liberal terms to induce the laborers to remain on the estates, they commenced, shortly after emancipation, a system of giving less wages, and exacting more work; and when the laborers retired from estate to field work, they were summarily ejected from the houses and lands they occupied on the estates, and their provision grounds were destroyed. The emancipated laborers had, therefore, no resource left but to separate themselves from the planting interest. Five-sixths of them became proprietors of from one to ten acres, which they now own, and which they grow in provisions for themselves and families. To supply other wants, they give casual labor to the estates; but they are free of the estates, and can work for whom they deem the best paymaster. If any doubts that a very large number, a very astonishing number, of the emancipated laborers have become independent proprietors, let him look at the score of villages built up since abolition, and so thickly scattered throughout the cultivated districts of Trinidad that it would be superfluous in me to point them out."

"Antigua hastened in advance of all other colonies to emancipate her slaves. She refused to believe in the virtues of an apprenticeship, or in the doctrine that her bondmen needed a purgatory to prepare them for freedom. Her rulers were wise in their generation. They foresaw that with the substitution of free labor for slave labor much had to be learned, and much to be unlearned; that the success of the new system could only be determined by time and experience; and that an early start in the race was a point to be gained, not to be neglected. Antigua has never had any cause to regret the independent course she then thought proper to pursue. * * * The improved condition of the peasantry is never doubted or questioned in the island itself, and it is well shown by the nature and extent of the imports during late years, as compared with their nature and extent before emancipation. From 1822 to 1832, the average annual value of goods imported by Antigua was £130,000 sterling; in 1858, the island imported to the value of £266,364 sterling. During ten years preceding emancipation, the average number of vessels that annually entered the different ports of the island was 340, and the tonnage 30,000. In 1858, the number of vessels was 668, and the tonnage 42,534. In 1846, there were in the island 67 villages, containing 3187 houses and 9033 inhabitants. All these villages were founded, and all these houses built, since emancipation. In 1858, 2000 additional houses had been built, and the number of village residents had risen to 15,644. At the same period, there were only 299 paupers in the island. The planters of Antigua avow, what is unquestionably true, that by the introduction of a cheaper system of labor, the island was saved, in 1834, from impending ruin."

"With regard to Jamaica, I do not mean to say that the estates have anything like a sufficiency of labor. I merely wish to give point-blank denial to a very general impression, that the Jamaica negroes will not work at all. Nine out of ten rely principally upon their own properties for the support of themselves and their families; but they are willing, nevertheless, to work for the estates, or on the roads, when it does not interfere with necessary labor on their own lands. When the choice lies between the roads and the estates, it is not surprising that they should select the employer that *pays best and most regularly.* The Jamaica negro gives as much labor, even to the sugar estates, as he consistently can, and it is no fault of his if he cannot give enough. They are a peaceable, law-abiding peasantry, with whom the remembrance of past wrongs has had so little weight that, from the day of emancipation until now, they have never dreamed of a hostile combination, either against their old masters, or the government under which they live; though in the time of slavery, insurrections were numerous and terrible. The condition of the Jamaica peasants in 1860 is a standing rebuke to those who, wittingly or unwittingly, encourage the vulgar lie, that the African cannot possibly be elevated. The dissolute idlers, loafers, and vagabonds, that congregate in Kingston and other towns, are as different from their country brethren, as the rowdy of New York city is different from the honest farmers of the State."

COMPARATIVE CHEAPNESS OF FREE LABOR.

"N Barbadian planter, in 1859, would hesitate to select free labor in preference to slave labor, as in his belief the more economical of the two. Every planter in Jamaica knows from his own books, if they go back far enough, that free labor is cheaper than slave labor. He knows that the cultivation of an acre of cane does not now cost him $40, when in other times it cost him $80. He knows that under slavery, the digging an acre of cane-holes cost from $35 to $45, while under freedom it is from $8 to $15. He knows that under one system 30 per cent. of his laboring force were non effectives, and had to be fed and clothed like the rest; while under freedom no work is paid for that is not actually performed. He knows that a free laborer is not bought, and that the sum he would cost can be otherwise laid out at profitable interest. He knows that it is no longer necessary to make allowance of ten or even fifteen per cent. for death or depreciation. These are facts readily admitted, and whoever takes the trouble to think will see their force."

"If I were asked to point out the chief obstruction to a satisfactory solution of the West India labor question, I should answer, without hesitation, want of confidence between employer and employed. The planters cling unwittingly to the shreds of the system of coercion in which they were once taught to believe. They do not yet recognize the overwhelming advantages of perfectly free labor; for they have checked its development, by imposing upon it some of the heaviest burdens of feudalism and of serfdom. They do not seem to reflect for a moment that the interest of a proprietor is to elevate, not to degrade, his laborer. They have misjudged the negro throughout, and have put too much faith in his supposed inferiority. After the important step of emancipation was taken, they did little to turn it to the best account."

"I came to the West Indies imbued with the American idea, that African freedom had been a curse to every branch of agricultural and commercial industry. I shall leave these islands overwhelmed with a very opposite conviction. I deny that the negroes lack industry, when by industry they can add to their means, or advance their prosperity. The more I saw, the more I became convinced that *debt and want of capital*, much more than want of *labor*, had led to the abandonment of so many estates; and be it always remembered, that *the burden of debt was incurred before freedom was tested*. Freedom, when allowed fair play, has injured none of these colonies. It saved them from a far deeper and more lasting depression than any they have yet known. It was a boon conferred upon all classes of society; upon planter and laborer; upon commerce and agriculture; upon industry and education; upon morality and religion. If a perfect measure of success remains to be achieved, let not freedom be condemned; for the obstacles to overcome were great, and the workers were few and unwilling. If I can stimulate inquiry on a subject so important, and so widely misunderstood as the West India labor question, I shall have achieved all the success at which I have aimed."

EMANCIPATION IN THE WEST INDIES.

A public meeting was held at Willis's Rooms, London, on Wednesday, Feb. 20th, 1861, to receive a report from E. B. Underhill, Esq., and the Rev. J. T. Brown, the deputation of the Baptist Missionary Society, of their recent visit to the West Indies. Charles Buxton, Esq., M. P., took the chair at twelve o'clock.

The CHAIRMAN said it must be remembered that, in the time of slavery, whatever the island produced was exported; the food of the slaves consisting principally of salt fish and yams, their clothes and lodging being of the most wretched description. At the present time, however, the creoles were rapidly rising in their social and physical condition, and appropriated, to a great extent, the productions of the country for their own use. He would not anticipate the report of the deputation, but would simply add that, in his opinion, notwithstanding every discouragement, emancipation had proved itself, beyond all doubt, to be a good thing for Jamaica, not only by producing glorious moral results, but by enormously enhancing the prosperity of the island.

Mr. UNDERHILL said Mr. Brown and himself proceeded towards the close of 1859 to the West Indies. Mr. Brown spent, altogether, about six months in Jamaica, and he (Mr. Underhill) about a year, in that and the other islands of the West Indies; and therefore the statements they were prepared to make were the result of no rapid and cursory view, but of close investigation, followed out to the best of their ability. He would not attempt to make a speech calculated to move their feelings; but, having laid before them some bare facts, he would leave these facts to tell their own tale. He must admit that, at the first show of things, those who maintained that emancipation had failed had something in their favor. There could be no question that, with regard to Jamaica, there had been a very considerable diminution in the exportation of the staple products of the country. The exportation of sugar had, for instance, declined from 1,400,000 cwt. in 1831 — three years before the passing of the first Act of Emancipation — to 535,000 cwt. in 1858. The exportation of rum also had declined from 35,000 puncheons in 1833 to 18,000 in 1858. In coffee the reduction was still more manifest, since whereas in 1830 the island exported 22,000,000 lbs., in 1858 it only exported 5,250,000 lbs. He must also admit that upon entering the island of Jamaica, the representations as to its decline struck one as being very truthful. On landing at Kingston, one found a large city, the streets of which were either deep in mud or sand. The whole town appeared sadly neglected, and many large warehouses were wholly unoccupied, whilst beggars and drunkards abounded. The feeling of depression was still further increased upon reading the newspapers, or going into the country. Estates, once flourishing, were desolate and uncultivated, and the buildings in every direction were rapidly falling into decay. But there were one or two circumstances which materially altered the first impression which this state of things produced on the mind. In the first place, while Jamaica, to use a favorite expression, had been ruined, the West Indies generally had prospered. It was a curious fact, for instance, that while the exportation of sugar for three years before emancipation had averaged from all the islands 3,000,000 cwts., in 1858 it amounted to 3,500,000 cwts., being only a diminution of 100,000 cwts., or about 2,000 hogsheads. It was obvious, therefore, that there was some other cause for the decay of Jamaica. Then, with regard to coffee, it must be remembered that Ceylon had thrown an immense quantity of that commodity into the English market. For example, in 1839 Ceylon exported 4,500,000 lbs. of coffee, whereas sixteen years afterwards it actually exported 56,000,000 lbs. (Hear, hear.) That would partly account for the decline of the production of that commodity in Jamaica. With regard to Kingston, also, he learnt that instead of being, as it once was, a kind of central market for the Spanish Main, the merchants of the different ports in South America either stopped at St. Thomas's island, or preferred to trade direct with Europe, which would account largely for the appearance of Kingston. It must also be remembered that the trade in Kingston had changed from being principally wholesale to a retail character, so that while, on the one hand, it had suffered by the diminution of the former, it had gained by the increase of the latter. He would proceed to show what was the condition of the general population in Jamaica. There were 380,000 people in the island, and dependant to a great extent on the cultivation of the land. These people were the slaves of former days, but were now the enfranchised peasantry, and it was only right to consider how emancipation had affected their interests. On this point he could at once say that their position had in every respect immensely improved. It had been said that the negroes were an idle lot of people, who squatted upon the land, and were quite content if they got a pumpkin to eat. But this was quite false. The first thing the negroes did was to leave the estates in great numbers. There were now but few estates on which they resided, and in those cases the planters had treated them as free men, and consequently secured their affections and services. A contrary line of treatment was pursued in the majority of instances, and that, together with want of capital wherewith to pay the wages weekly, had the effect of driving them away. The slaves who thus left the estates were compelled to seek other means of subsistence, but they did not "squat upon the land," as had been alleged — that is, settle upon it without paying rent. The circumstance that nearly every inch of land in Jamaica was owned by some one made such a thing impossible.

On the contrary, great numbers of the old slaves had purchased land, and it was an amazing fact that, at this moment, three-fifths of the cultivated land in Jamaica was the *bona fide* property of the blacks. (Applause.) He held in his hand a return of one mission congregation, and there were some interesting facts contained in it which he would take the liberty of quoting. In that congregation there were seventy-three heads of families, of whom sixty-two were once slaves, which should be charitably considered when looking at the progress they have made in the arts of civilization and mental culture. It could not be expected that in twenty-one years all the old feelings and passions and moral taints of slavery would be removed from the land. These seventy-three families possessed among them 342 acres of freehold land, and rented an average of two acres each besides. They possessed amongst them seventy horses or mules — a species of property negroes were very anxious to have. Surely these facts proved that they were not "squatters," in the sense in which that word was used. The report of the Hanover Agricultural Society strongly supported him in the conclusions to which he had arrived in reference to the negro population. That report stated that in six districts of the parish, containing four or five thousand people, there were 802 proprietors, holding about 4,200 acres amongst them, which would be about five and a-half acres to each family. He valued the land possessed by the people at 3*l*. 10s. per acre, which was a much lower estimate than he might fairly put upon it. This would make 1,050,000*l*. as the price they had paid for the land. But they had not only bought land — they had built houses upon it. The cottages in which they lived during slavery had been destroyed, and he was thankful it was so. The people had built for themselves a better class of houses, at a cost which could not be less than 10*l*. per house, and he was very glad to say it was very rare to find more than one family in a house. That amounted at least to 600,000*l*. Their furniture would be very moderately valued at 3*l*. per house — about half the real value — making an additional 180,000*l*.; and their carts, horses, mules, pigs, &c., could not be put at less than 50,000*l*., which was, in fact, much under the mark. The next item was a very interesting one, namely, the value of the sugar-mills, and implements used in the production of sugar. There were 143 sugar-mills in a portion of Hanover alone, and there could not be less than 5,000 in the island of Jamaica. These mills were valued by the Hanover Agricultural Society at 10*l*. each. Then, as to their clothes, they were as well dressed as the agricultural laborers of England, and every negro had at least one if not two suits. It was not true that the moral and respectable people were gaudily dressed. Upon the whole, the clothes would be cheaply valued at 1*l*. per head — making 380,000*l*. Then, and lastly, there were deposits in the savings' banks to the extent of 49,305*l*. The sum total of all this property, which had been accumulated since the emancipation, was 2,358,000*l*. — an estimate which he ventured to say was much below the mark. Of course there were some idle and some ragged people among them, as, indeed, there were in every country on the face of the earth. But, at any rate, it would be very unfair to take Kingston as a fair sample of the island. It only numbered 30,000 people out of a population of 380,000, and it would never do to judge of a people by the minority. The annual value of the exports from Jamaica, taking an average of three years, was 1,057,000*l*., including sugar, rum, coffee, and the other products of the island, but it must not be supposed that the whole of that was grown by white people. It might be purchased and owned by the whites, but the work had been done by black hands, and directed by black heads. He found that each family cultivated some land for itself — say an acre to each family. An acre would produce from 15*l*. to 50*l*. worth per annum; he had estimated it at 20*l*. The entire produce of this island would be 2,500,000*l*. per annum. Was that an idle people? His calculations were checked in a very interesting way by those of the Hanover Agricultural Society, to which he had previously alluded. That society estimated the average earnings of each family at 30*l*. per annum. The number of families was 76,000, so that, according to the society, the annual earnings of the negroes in Jamaica amounted to 2,280,000*l*., a conclusion nearly similar to his own, though he had arrived at it by a totally different process of calculation. Another interesting feature was the decrease which had taken place in the importation of salt fish. In the days of slavery the yam and salt fish constituted the chief food of the people, but now there was a growing taste for fresh meat, and many planters were turning their property into pens for the breeding and fattening of cattle. One black man, who was formerly a slave, but who now carried on the business of butcher in one of the towns, told him that in Christmas week he had killed nine head of cattle, and the returns of his business amounted to 5,000*l*. a year, though there were two other butchers in the same town. In one town — the town which owed its existence almost entirely to Mr. Knibb — from five to seven head of cattle were slaughtered every week. All these things showed that the people were advancing in their social condition.

A few facts might not be uninteresting with reference to the religious condition of the people. In the first place they had built 220 chapels, quite independent of the Established Church, of which he could find no record showing their number. In connection with these chapels there were 53,000 communicants, or about one-eighth of the entire population. This itself was a very gratifying and rather unusual state of things. The number of people regularly attending these chapels was 91,000, or about a fourth part of the population, and the Sunday-schools contained about 22,000 children, or about a third of the children who were capable of attending school. Lastly, they raised every year for religious purposes about 22,000*l.*

Crime was rare in the West Indies — he meant crime which brought men to the courts of law. He found from the published returns, that the number of men in prison during 1854 was 908, whilst the number in prison at one time in 1858 was only 600. That was not a very considerable number for so large a population. The people were very fond of cutlasses, and there was hardly a man who had not got one, but yet one scarcely ever heard of a cutlass being used to the injury of another man. Men had been known to throw away their cutlasses when they have been quarrelling, lest they should be tempted to use them against each other — a cirumstance which showed a great amount of self-control, and accounted for the unfrequency of great crimes. There was a rising feeling in favor of marriage, and an increasing respect for the marriage tie amongst the negroes since the abolition of slavery. True, the feeling was not yet so prevalent as could be wished, but the missionaries were doing all they could to encourage it. The question of education was one of vast importance in relation to the negro. The progress made in the island in this respect had been slight, but from a census taken by one of the missionaries at an interval of twenty-five years, he found that whereas just before freedom only three negroes in 5,000 could be found in one particular district that could read and write, at the next census 1,700 were able to do so. That showed that some progress had been made, but for all that the great want of Jamaica was education. The conclusion he had come to was this, that though emancipation might have occasioned some difficulties to the planters, it had been an unmixed blessing to the people. He did not know a single drawback or qualification that need be made to that statement. Should the planters continue in their present course, they also would reap the advantage in the general peace and security of the country, and in their own increased pecuniary gains. Last of all, he believed the tide in Jamaica was now turned, and that ordinary foresight, prudence, and care might make the island even more prosperous in years to come than it had ever been in the past. He recalled his visit to Jamaica with sincere pleasure. He went with deep trembling, but had come away with a gladdened heart, satisfied — as he trusted the meeting was, after having the facts he had laid before it — that Jamaica had not suffered from emancipation, but that its results, both to the people and to their country, would prove to be of the highest, most blessed, and most advantageous kind. (Applause.)

The Rev. J. T. BROWN said he rose with a very great deal of pleasure to add a few words to those which his friend and colleague had addressed to the meeting. He concurred in the statements of his colleague as to the social results which had flowed from emancipation; and he could, if he had time, adduce many facts in their corroboration; but there were many doubtless in that meeting who felt, with him, that whilst the social welfare of a people was a good thing, yet that their religious welfare was paramount, and that if they could not have brought good tidings in that respect, they must have come home indeed with a heavy heart. One source of difficulty in judging of the state of Jamaica was the fact that false reports of the land were circulated by disappointed planters, by bigots, by clever writers, and by disheartened missionaries. What the *Times* newspaper chose to say upon the subject was, to a great extent, matter of indifference, because every one knew what worth to attach to it; but when he saw a statement so utterly untrue as that contained in the " Encyclopædia Britannica,"—he did not impute wilful falsehood to the writer,—he was grieved indeed. That statement was to the effect that, during slavery, the Dissenting ministers possessed great influence over the negro, but that the latter now preferred the Established Church, because it cost him nothing, though, in point of fact, he cared but little for either. This was altogether a misrepresentation. (Great cheering.) One of the last persons who had contributed to this popular error was that clever writer of fiction, Mr. Trollope, who deserved to be described as a writer of fiction, not only as the author of " Barchester Towers " and " Framley Parsonage," but of the book he had published on the West Indies. ("Hear, hear," and laughter.) Whenever persons in Jamaica wished to represent a violent, prejudiced, and obstinate person,— one who judged as hastily of a religious body as Mr. Trollope judged of the Baptists,— who would rather dance with a Jew than pray with a Baptist, when they wished to speak of a person of violent and prejudiced character, looking only at one side of a question, running and jumping through a country,— one, in fact, who was altogether untrustworthy,—they would say of him that he had been " Trollopeing." (Laughter.) That was the name Mr. Trollope had given to such a character in Jamaica. But facts were facts, and, though Mr. Trollope avowed his dislike for statistics, there were some very stubborn ones which stared him in the face. In the first place, the people were orderly in their conduct — well governed and well behaved; persons and property were perfectly safe on the island, and serious crimes were very rare. The marriage tie was respected, and children respected their parents. These were facts which forcibly contrasted with the awful condition of society before the emancipation. Again, the religious statistics of the country spoke loudly in favor of emancipation. They contributed largely towards the expenses of religious worship, and many attended punctually the means of grace. The European Dissenting ministers on the island received 150*l.* per annum, and the native preachers, of whom there were sixteen, from 100*l.* to 120*l.* per annum. There were seventy-seven churches connected with the Baptist body in the island ; these included 20,000 communicants and 2,000 anxious inquirers ; and although there were at times instances of false profession and cases of backsliding, yet the discipline of the churches was good, and their condition altogether in many respects furnished good examples for Christian congregations at home. He could not forbear also paying a high tribute to the deacons and elders, who, taken upon the whole, were a fine body of Christian disciples, and true helpers of the ministry. He was aware that there was a great deal of mental ignorance in the island, but even in that respect its condition had materially improved since the emancipation. He wished many of the persons now listening to him could have listened to the speeches of some of the Christian negroes at some of their meetings in Jamaica, and have marked the strong common sense and great intelligence which tumbled awkwardly out of their mouths ; or could have heard their prayers, where beautiful thoughts and clear and holy aspirations struggled through their broken speech — indications of a mental vigor which only needed cultivation, and which even now commanded respect.

The Rev. WILLIAM ARTHUR then moved the following resolution : —

"That this meeting has heard with great pleasure the satisfactory account given by the deputation of the Baptist Missionary Society of the results of emancipation in the West Indies, and Jamaica in particular, and of the progress made by the negro population in civilization, intelligence, and piety, and deem the great Act of Emancipation of 800,000 slaves, an act just and right in itself, as amply vindicated by the success which has attended it."

He felt it to be a real honor to be asked to move this resolution, and he congratulated the Baptist Missionary Society on having sent out so able a deputation to the West Indies. Their report was a most important one, and the more so at this juncture, when the attention of the people of America was anxiously directed to the results of emancipation in the West Indies, and especially in Jamaica. The friends of freedom had reason to be deeply thankful to Mr. Underhill for his careful and comprehensive inquiry into the real state of affairs.

The Rev. EDWARD MATHEWS, in seconding the resolution, said that he could testify from his own experience in the State of Ohio that the facts adduced by the deputation would have much influence in America, and help forward the cause of emancipation there.

www.ingramcontent.com/pod-product-compliance
Lightning Source LLC
Chambersburg PA
CBHW030408170426
43202CB00010B/1529